Lifestyles of the Rich & Righteous

God's will in earth as it is in heaven

Pastor Katrine Forbes

Bloomington, IN  Milton Keynes, UK

authorHOUSE

AuthorHouse™
1663 Liberty Drive, Suite 200
Bloomington, IN 47403
www.authorhouse.com
Phone: 1-800-839-8640

AuthorHouse™ UK Ltd.
500 Avebury Boulevard
Central Milton Keynes, MK9 2BE
www.authorhouse.co.uk
Phone: 08001974150

First published by AuthorHouse 7/12/2006

ISBN: 1-4259-1662-7 (sc)

Library of Congress Control Number: 2006900889

Printed in the United States of America
Bloomington, Indiana

This book is printed on acid-free paper.

Table of Contents

DEDICATION

Dedicated to the memory of Allen L. Forbes,

The most gentle and kind son born to any parents,

loved by everyone and gone too soon.

I am eternally grateful for the time God gave us with him.

His encouragement to me, and his love of ministry and family

will be remembered forever.

His beauty truly is his kindness.

ACKNOWLEDGEMENTS

I am as always, thankful to my husband and friend for life Elder David Forbes Sr. Your unending support in the ministry and encouragement has been invaluable to me. There is no other person I would want to live my dreams with. I am also forever grateful for the spiritual warfare that began over 45 years ago by my sister and mother-in-the-Lord, Dr. Cora Lee Palmer. Thank you for your continued prayers and fasting, and for being there when I needed you. Your life has been a shinning example of obedience and sacrifice.

No one person can be more responsible for my stand for true Holiness than my mentor and teacher in the Gospel, Mother Anna A. Stevenson; a woman that epitomized integrity, strength and the character of Christ. Although she no longer resides on earth, the footprint of her teachings will remain with me forever. To my daughter Viola, thank you for professionally translating the spirit of the spoken word to the printed page, and for bringing my sermons and my vision to life. Your work has been extremely helpful in enabling me to complete this project.

My inspiration to reach higher and dig deeper for truth is stimulated by the loyal people of Now Faith Ministries. Thank you for your confidence in me and your spirit of obedience.

PREFACE

*I*n Lifestyles of the Rich and Righteous we are dealing with balance. Presently the church is divided between two prevalent beliefs. On one hand we have the "faith-based" doctrine, which embraces the teaching of prosperity. In contrast to that, we have the "service" based doctrine, which concentrates on prayer, praise, worship and service.

If either of these doctrines focuses solely on these components the church experiences a serious void. The two doctrines must be inclusive of each other for true faith, worship and praise to be given to our heavenly Father. The balance of these two equally important truths will be at the forefront of our focus in this revealing book.

Of course Holiness is not a dress, a house or a car, and it is also not a scripture or a song. Holiness is Jesus Christ and only through worshiping Him in spirit and in truth will everything else as a consequence, be added to you. It is our Father's good pleasure to give us the Kingdom which lacks absolutely nothing. The Kingdom of God has an inexhaustible supply of wealth – as well as praises to God. Gaining an understanding of this balance is the focus of

Lifestyles of the Rich and Righteous. With a well-balanced composition of the whole truth, the Body of Christ can experience living lifestyles rich in earthly treasures as well as heavenly. This book is not about my will being accomplished, it's about God's will. This book will reveal through the exploration in scriptures that God's will is for His Kingdom to come, on earth as it is in heaven …in our lifetime.

INTRODUCTION

*A*ccording to Fortune Magazine Oprah Winfrey has reached the pinnacle of success and is now at the helm of a billion-dollar empire. It was actually reported at 988 million but who's counting. Rapper/entrepreneur Percy Miller (Master P) was ranked 20th on Fortune's Top 40 Under 40. At the age of 33 Miller was worth a cool $249 million and has one room in his house that is worth more than my entire house. If you think that's impressive then perhaps it goes without saying that Mr. Gates, William G. Gates, that is, CEO of Microsoft, his net worth is estimated to be $54 billion in 2002. He now ranks as the richest man in the world. Professional athletes own anywhere from one to eight vehicles with an average price tag of $60,000 each. Movie stars fly in private jets that cost $15,000 to rent for a couple of hours. They have homes all across the globe from Monte Carlo to California, and believe it or not reservations have even been made for the moon as soon as they work out that little gravity problem.

The knowledge of their wealth conjured up fond memories of a once famous TV show of the 1980's. The name of the show was Lifestyles of the Rich and Famous. Robin Leach who talked about champagne wishes and caviar dreams hosted the show. I used to watch the show because of all the beautiful homes and cars that I saw. Amazingly, from age seventeen to seventy, one celebrity after another sported their extravagances and bling-bling for the whole world to see.

Week after week, I waited with anticipation for someone, anyone to offer the slightest praise to God for their wealth and affluence. I would have even settled for the obligatory "thanks to the man upstairs" which happens to be extremely popular these days. Although, we did get a lot of "knock on woods" – a poor substitute for a public profession or for giving sincere thanks to God. Most of the rich and famous appeared to be like the rich man in the New Testament that laid up all his treasures on earth. He had every earthly possession imaginable but the mere thought of relinquishing them kept him from getting into heaven. Riches alone will never satisfy man's need for relationship with the Father.

On the flip side of this there's the Christian who is trying to squeeze a dollar out of fifty cents and feels it is giving glory to God. They feel it is all a part of the required suffering guaranteeing them entrance into heaven. These people think it admirable to struggle, and wear their burdens like a badge of honor. Just making it is also not our Father's desire for His children.

Americans were wooed every week as Hollywood opened its doors to us for a glimpse of the stars living in ways that we could only dream of. But their wealth was no dream - It is undeniable, the rich and famous are super rich. Some are so rich that that they don't have a clue what to do with their money. This is never more evident than when one actresses' pooch is carried around in a dog carrier by Asprey and Garrard valued at $19,000, and a rapper owns over fifty cars and five stretch limousines. Yes, they are rich, but Jesus taught us that it was unbalanced for a man to gain the whole world and lose his soul. And in fact, he really hasn't profited at all (Matthew 16:26 KJV). How many of today's celebrities do we know that have committed or attempted to commit suicide?

How many have drug and alcohol addictions or are just plain loony? It's not enough to have money. Money's only byproduct is the houses, the cars, the clothes and the jewelry. At the end of the day that's all they have to show for themselves. They are left unsatisfied and empty. This is because they do not know Jesus Christ. They have not experienced His peace. They can not testify about His love. From the outside looking in, it seems as if they have everything. Everything except the one thing that matters the most – Christ.

Chapter One

I AM COMING OUT OF THIS!

*Y*our present position does not dictate your ultimate location. You can start from where you are right now - to get anywhere you want to be. All of your previous hopes and dreams may have been doomed to failure, but failure is not a reflection of your greatness.

How many Americans know that world famous left-handed slugger, Babe Ruth - struck out over thirteen hundred times? Not many, because his accomplishments outweigh his failures. What we do remember, is the overwhelming end of his career story – the Babe holds the record for the highest slugging percentage in Major League history.

We don't hold it against Michael Jordan for retiring from basketball in 1993, only to change his mind later and appear in minor league baseball for an embarrassing, short-lived run. We forgave his indecision, because he more than redeemed himself later – leaving us a legacy worthy of remembering. His Airness ranks today as the number one basketball player of all time, which is more than memorable.

Or does it matter, that World Champion Russian figure skating pair – Tatiana Totmianina and her partner Maxim, suffered the devastation of her falling face first to the ice in 2004? That may be memorable, but not as memorable as what happened later. The couple went on to become number one in the world in 2005. Not many people recall these catastrophic failures, because they really don't matter.

The beginning of your story isn't important to God. No matter how hopeless that story may be. Hopelessness is no match for the rescuing power of God. All through the Bible, some of the most remarkable victories were wrought through disastrous beginnings. It is the end of the matter that really matters.

Genesis chapters 38-42 gives us the true story of a memorable beginning and an even more unforgettable ending. Here, a precocious young boy found himself in a terribly disastrous situation. His memorable yet insignificant beginnings take us back about two thousand years before Christ in the land of Canaan. A rich man by the name of Jacob had twelve sons and one daughter. Of his thirteen children he loved Joseph best of all. Joseph was a young boy about the age of seventeen, and he had a dream. The fulfillment of this dream would eventually lead to the deliverance of the children of Israel. For this reason Joseph was always noted in the Bible as a type of Savior.

One day he had the most unusual dream, and he felt compelled to share it with his brothers. Some people think that he made a mistake by telling his brothers because of what came of it in the end. It actually was not a mistake, because a righteous man's steps are ordered by the Lord according to Psalms 37:23 KJV. And Joseph was indeed a righteous man. Would they have ever known that the prophecy in the dream came to pass - had he not told them in advance? God ordained Joseph to tell the dream to his brothers. He told them of the dream in which there were twelve stalks of grain and eleven of the stalks bowed down to one. The outcome of the dream was that Joseph was exalted and his bothers had to give allegiance to him. His brothers didn't like this because they were jealous. It's not unusual that we see the provocation of jealousy here, perhaps brought about by God Himself.

The God of all knowing could choose anything He wants to stimulate us for His desired ending. We will see in the chapters to follow – how God had to choose something more powerful than death to motivate His people for a desired end.

The Bible shows us that Joseph's big brothers were jealous because God honored Joseph. The love of the Father still continues to be a cause of jealousy for people today. Even the love of a natural father causes jealous sibling rivalries that go on for a lifetime. Jacob loved his son so much that he made Joseph a coat of many colors to pay homage to him. Now his brothers really envied him.

A couple of days later Jacob sent the boys out to graze the flock. He kept Joseph at home to be with him. Doesn't that beat all! Joseph, the younger and more cerebral baby brother - gets to stay home with daddy and his Crayola colored coat - while the elder brothers labor with the flock. This looks to his brothers like they're being punished. To a certain extent, it really is the opportunity of a lifetime, to honorably become caregivers, shepherds to a hungry and needy flock. The very animal that would be the symbolism of our savior. But these guys weren't into feeding anything but their ego-starved personalities. After a few days he decided to send Joseph to check on his brothers. The Bible says Dan saw his brother coming in the distance. He said to the others, "Here comes the dreamer." Filled with indignation, they rolled their eyes, and were ready to pack up and leave before Joseph got there.

"Look at him." Levi said. "He thinks he is better than us with that stupid coat." The rest mumbled their agreement. "Hey, let's kill him." Levi suggested. "Then we'll be rid of him for good." He snickered. This idea interested the brothers. Joseph had done nothing but caused them trouble since the day he was born.

"We can not kill him." shouted Ruben, the oldest and the voice of reason. "With our own brother's blood on our hands we'd be cursed for the rest of lives."

"So what'll we do?" Levi countered quickly. "Should we just let him torture us for the rest of our lives?" "Our father will give his whole inheritance to Joseph, and you, the oldest, won't get a thing." Levi taunted.

Levi wasn't concerned about Reuben's inheritance – he was concerned about his own. The laws of inheritance were clear. It required that all the male siblings would divide their father's wealth equally. It was their unmentioned sister Dinah that Levi should have shown pity for. People often disguise their true self-seeking intentions with a false sense of concern for your well-being. Ruben considered this for a moment, figuring that Levi was probably right, he said to his brothers, "Let's throw him in this pit, and leave him." They agreed that this was the best alternative.

"Shhh, Be quiet – here comes the dreamer" whispered Gad fearing the boy would overhear their deadly plans.

They took him and put him in the pit as they had planned. As Joseph felt the tears well up in his eyes, and as the hopelessness of his predicament settled in on him, he knew that he was coming out of that pit. While preparing for this sermon, I was personally facing family and financial problems, as well as carrying the weight of the problems of my congregation. Right then and there, Holy Ghost boldness came over me as I thought about the pitfalls I was facing. Out of the depths of my soul came a prophetic word of knowledge… with no regard for who was listening I shouted, **"I - Am – coming – out - of - this!"** Even then, in the privacy of my prayer quarters, Satan tried to tempt me with the awkwardness of such a silly proclamation. Silliness aside, you must openly and verbally pronounce the commencement of deliverance from your pit. Satan does not want you to receive your deliverance! Any opportunity given him to kill, steal or destroy, he will take it.

The circumstances of life, at one time or another has made us all feel like Joseph – buried alive in a pit. For many of us it's a pit of debt. You may feel like you are in a grave, smothered by all kinds of things. While in the "hole" you too can declare the commencement of your deliverance - that you are coming out of this! Out of the depths of your spirit, you must dig down deeper than the pit or hole you're in, and say I - Am - coming - out - of - this!

While Joseph was in the pit he thought of all the prophecies that God had showed him and this proved to be a source of his contentment. When you steadfastly affirm your faith that God will come through, you will gain assurance. Joseph told himself, "I don't know when or how I'm coming out of this, but I am coming out. His brothers left him for dead but he refused to die. The Devil (your adversary) attempts to destroy you with the power of words. Use the power of your words to destroy his works.

The most powerful combination of words in the English Language is "I" and "Am". When you say, "I Am", you identify yourself with God all mighty. Pharaoh had the children of Israel in bondage. God told Moses to go and tell Pharaoh to *let* His people go. Moses asked God, "Who should I say sent me?" God said don't worry about that. Just tell him *I Am* sent you (Exodus 3:14 KJV). When you say *I Am* and *I Will* you identify yourself with the Trinity. When you say I am coming out of this you are refusing to be buried with troubles of this life. You internally declare that you will not stop living before you die. The mere assertion of I Am gives power and intensity to a believer's pit situations. You are using what God used to deliver His people out of their pit. God intends for his earthly image to pattern themselves after their heavenly likeness. He used I Am – because he wants you to use I Am.

In the Gospel of John Jesus emphatically declares his exclusivity by using I AM. He does it in a way that it resonates eternally. He was a master of words, a creator of language and he could have chosen another phrasing, but nothing could assert His meaning better than I AM. In these passages, He states His position of power as being the ONLY one, not one of the ones.

Check out how He enlightens the world:

I AM the bread of life, John 6:35

I AM the light of the world, John 8:12

I AM the door, John 10:9

I AM come to give life more abundantly, John10:10

I AM the good shepherd, John 10:11 & 14

I AM the son of God, John 10:36

I AM the resurrection, John 11:25

I AM the way, the truth and the life, John, 14:6

I AM the true vine John, 15:1

The spirit of I AM lives in us. Whatever perilous situation
you are in - you must declare I AM coming out of it.

That's just what Joseph did. He was left in the pit for dead, but
he came out of that pit. Later, a group of Midianites stopped to
try and barter with his brothers. Joseph, of course, heard this and
started up his screaming again. Do you care that your critics say
you're screaming like a girl? Or that you can't take anything. Be
like Joseph, disregard the critics and shout for your deliverance
even in the face of danger.

"What is that?" One of the men asked.

"Nothing." Gad said quickly.

"Nothing huh? We'll get rid of that "nothing" for eight ounces of
silver." Suddenly, Gad's greed radar went off the meter. Because
that was way more than the nothing they would get if they had
killed Joseph.

"Okay go ahead." He said. So they sold their brother into slavery for a measly two bags of silver.

Joseph had escaped one pit only to be cast into another. He was probably wondering what he had done to deserve such a fate. What he did not know was that his journey was far from over and God was granting him a divine test of his faith. We've all heard it said before…there is no glory without a story and the story of Joseph is a miraculous one.

The Midianites took Joseph to Egypt and he was sold to Potiphar, an officer to the king of Egypt and captain of the palace guard. Despite being Potiphar's servant Joseph found favor in the eyes of Potiphar and was given charge over everything that Potiphar owned. Regardless of his "position" as a slave Joseph was living comfortably. Instead of being treated like a servant, he was treated more like a partner. Joseph was thinking that this isn't so bad. In fact, he was living just as well as Potiphar was.

God had given Joseph favor. The Bible says God blessed Joseph and all that were associated with him. God gave him favor and honor in prison. Contrary to popular opinion, God's divine favor is not manifested because things are well with you. The divine opposite is true. You don't need divine favor for your finances when you already have millions in the bank. When you're at the height of your career, or you've achieved the pinnacle of success and your name is a household word – it's hard to fathom the need for divine favor. But when the time comes that your name is mud and your and your outlook is worse - Divine favor allows safe passage for believers to overcome satanic obstructions.

Divine favor opens doors for those who could never own the key. It dispenses mercy above justice. God's favor miraculously emerges when the need is at its greatest. In your red seas, in your prisons, in your lion's Dens, in your fiery furnaces and in your personal pits - divine favor takes over and causes *every* power to surrender to the will of God for your advancement.

Potiphar's wife also found favor with Joseph. She thought the young handsome Hebrew was quite a catch. She looked on him and lusted after him. She put all her cards on the table with Joseph, but he was a righteous man of God and even as her slave, refused to let the devil steal his anointing. Joseph resisted her advances. This only managed to anger her. She decided to plot a scheme to get Joseph. He was destined to make history - but he refused to be a chapter in herstory.

Joseph was satisfied living in Potiphar's house, having authority over everything and having control, but that was not God's ultimate location for him. God wanted to take him higher. Potiphar's wife began to throw herself on Joseph. Anything Joseph wanted was within his reach just for the asking. She would be at the beck and call of her secret lover, if he would only give in. Her husband, the older and more experienced father figure was only bait for her devilish plan of adultery. She was no different than most adulterers, manufacturing excuses and blaming their spouses to free their guilty minds -so they could sin more freely. Her plan 'A' was failing miserably. Mrs. Potiphar would have to resort to more desperate measures. She reasoned that every young man's fantasy would be to conquer the older married woman. Not so for Joseph, a young man full of integrity he would never circum, though very tempting, the enticement of a married woman.

Realizing that her best efforts were not winning him over, the Egyptian temptress was enraged. When she went to grab Joseph - he thought about all of the honor and favor from God and man. Temptation was never this hard. Joseph was no sissy, but to avoid giving any room to the devil he bailed. As precious as his anointed coat was, he would have to leave it behind.

To keep his coat would mean his undoing – but to lose his soul was a fate worst than death. He would have to come out of it. He left his coat, but not his covering.

Joseph was symbolically saying, I Am coming out of this. The Bible says Potiphar's wife held onto his coat. She couldn't have the man she would settle for his coat. When her husband came in, there she stood crying and lying. She said to him, "The man that you exalted and promoted tried to rape me and I screamed."

Regrettably, Joseph was put back in jail. He didn't deserve it but he ended up back in the pit. You may be in a pit *not* of your own doing. You didn't do anything. You were innocent but you got into a hole. The Bible says that God was still with Joseph. The reality of the situation hit him like a ton of bricks. Never in a million years did he think that his life would turn out like this. This could not have been God's plan for his life. Certainly those dreams he had didn't mean that he would spend his life in jail. Could it be? Still he had to remain faithful. He couldn't let his situation get the better of him. In the midst of adversity he had to give thanks. He had to worship. He had to show forth praises unto God.

There was a baker and a butler there that were removed from Pharaoh's house. We could speculate them fleeing the house for reasons no different than Joseph. At least jail would mean they're still alive and out of the reach of the venomous black widow. They each had a dream that troubled them. There was Joseph faithfully running around in the dungeon, talking about his God, I can envision him just singing…Jehovah Jireh the God that sees ahead and makes provisions. He asked them why they weren't happy. They said they weren't happy because of the dreams they had.

Joseph said why would you be troubled? Don't you know that God could give you the interpretation of the dreams? He put no stake in himself. Joseph didn't offer the fact that he could interpret the dreams. He said there is a God that could interpret the dreams. The butler proceeded to tell his dream. He said I had a dream and there was a vine that stood before me and there were three branches and the three branches started to bloom. Then he said I was holding the king's cup. I squeezed the grapes into the cup and gave it to the king. He had dreamed that he was the king's cupbearer. The cupbearer is there to taste the wine before the king tastes it. If there is any poison in the wine the king lives and the cupbearer dies. That was the butler's job, but for some reason (obvious to everyone but the king) the butler offended the king, and was thrown into prison.

Joseph told him that he in fact had a good dream. He told him in three days he was coming out of that pit (prison). Joseph went on to tell him that the vines, the cups and the grapes represented that God would highly honor and favor him. Joseph told him that he would pour Pharaoh's wine again. He would be restored to his previous position in the palace.

The baker now comes to Joseph because there was good news for the butler. He told his dream to Joseph and in his dream three baskets were on his head filled with food. Then there were some black birds that came and ate all the food out of the top basket. The three baskets represented three days. Joseph told him that his dream was not good. In three days Pharaoh would call for him, cut off his head, and leave his body on a pole and the birds would eat his body.

How on earth do you find a diplomatic way to tell somebody about their impending doom? This poor guy wished he had never asked. Now he would be faced with the reality of his own mortality. It was bad enough when his life was in their hands – he would have to settle for his fate. But once you've been told how and when you're going to die; there's a sinking feeling when your fate is in your own hands. Now the responsibility is squarely on you. This must be what King Hezekiah felt, but he turned his face to God didn't he.

Joseph said to the butler as he left the prison three days later, "When you come to glory again please remember me. Tell the king to bring me out of here." Joseph now begins to realize that he was not in this mess because of anything he had done but because of destiny and purpose. In other words, for the very same reason his brothers pitted him in the first place - for the love of his Father. This time it was his Father in heaven.

You are not going to reach your destiny and purpose in life without the occasional mess, or the occasional pit. In the chapters to follow I will show you the inevitable "will haves" that naturally happen to us by virtue of living a life of righteousness. As the Apostle Paul taught, you *will* be troubled on every side but *not* distressed. You *will* be perplexed but *not* in despair. You *will* suffer persecution, but *not* be forsaken. You *will* be cast down, but *not* destroyed. You will not know what method He is going to use, or the people He will use, but you *will have* the assurance of the word of God that *He will* bring you out.

Sadly, the butler got out and was so happy, that he forgot Joseph. We have to remember that when God brings us out not to forget the people that prayed for us – while we were imprisoned. I will never forget Mother Anna A. Stevenson, she taught me true Biblical holiness. Don't have the butler's mentality, and forget your bridge or your strong tower.

Joseph just kept saying "I am coming out of this". He had no doubt. When man forgets you it is an opportunity for God to remember you. There is a revelation to bring you out.

In the mean time, Joseph was waiting to get news from the Butler, two years went by before he heard from him. Can you imagine all the hope that Joseph had, depending on a man to get him out of this? And there was no response. A whole two years went by. Don't give up on your dream. Champagne wishes and caviar dreams may not be within your immediate grasp. You may live on toast with jam and tea. Years may go by before your deliverance is manifested, but rest in the Lord and wait patiently on him - I Am is within you.

The Bible says that the King had a dream and he was expressing to the people his vision. He called for his magicians and interpreters but no one could tell him what it meant. Suddenly the butler remembered Joseph. Our God knows how to bring us out. He knows who has the position. He knows who has the wisdom. He knows who has the finances and He knows who has the positional power for the pit you're in.

The Butler finally tells the king about Joseph, and the king looked around and said "all my magicians couldn't tell me the meaning of my dream."

The king said to Joseph "I hear you interpret dreams". Joseph didn't take any of the glory. He told him that it was his God that gave him the knowledge to interpret dreams. He said to Pharaoh let your dream be known. So Pharaoh began to explain his dream to Joseph. He said he looked on the banks of the Nile and there were seven fat cows. They looked like they were ready to burst. Then he looked again on the banks of the Nile and he saw seven more cows. These were lean, skinny and puny. They looked like their bones where ready to poke through their skin. And the seven lean cows ate the seven fat cows.

Pharaoh also dreamt of a corn stalk that went up into the heavens and seven branches came from that corn stalk, but the east wind came and blew it away. He thought this was bad.

Joseph told him the meaning of the dreams he had. The seven that he saw in his dreams was God's perfect number and represented seven years. The seven fat cows represented seven years of prosperity and the seven lean cows represented seven years of famine. Joseph advises the king. "This is what I want you to do. I want you to choose a man." He didn't say here I am. Choose me." He said, "Choose a man in your kingdom that will be in control of all the wheat and all the corn, and choose men that can take care of all the wealth in the kingdom." The king thought of all the men in his kingdom that were not able to interpret his dreams. He chose Joseph to be in control because his God was able to interpret his dreams. He saw God in Joseph. He brought him out of prison and promoted him to be governor in Egypt. He wanted a man that had God's anointing. He ordered that the people bow down to Joseph.

Joseph came out with honor and glory. He came out majestically. Joseph was the man. He put a ring on Joseph's hand, and a chain on his neck. He put a kingly robe on him, replacing his coat now gone forever. He told him he would be next in power to himself, and God reigned through Joseph in Egypt.

Joseph ended up gaining far more than he gave. The seven years of prosperity passed, and the famine started all over the region. Back home the famine hit Jacob and his eleven sons. Jacob and his sons were sitting around assessing at the effects of the famine. Jacob told his sons to go to Egypt and buy some corn so that they would live and not die. Because of Joseph being able to interpret Pharaoh's dream Egypt was able to provide food for not only itself but also for the entire region. They left Benjamin with their dad and went to Egypt. When they came Joseph was in control and he saw the same ten men coming that had left him for dead years earlier. You have to be careful who and what you declare as say is dead. Those same dead folks may rise up again and save your life.

When Joseph saw his ten brothers come in, instantly he knew they were *his* brothers. Soon the memories of their life together flooded him. Joseph couldn't take it any longer. He went into a room and he wept. He wept sore. This is why Joseph is seen as a type of Christ. If it were some of us today we would never dispose of a chance to get back. We would have killed them or at least condemned them for sure, but Joseph filled with the love of God, didn't get angry. Joseph was so full of love he forgot the bad deeds that his brothers did to him. Two years before the famine God had given him twin sons. The first son was Manasseh. Manasseh means *my God has caused me to forget all of my toil*. What a magnificent Deliverance! Imagine coming out of the most trying situation of your life, and being served up a miracle so incredible that you forget the pain of the pit.

When God brings you out – He intends for you to forget the pain of your pit. It won't be your doing. Those haunting memories won't linger. God will make you forget all of your trouble, and all of your pain. Meshach, Shadrach, and Abednego were placed in the furnace of a consuming fire, and came out without even the scent of smoke on them (Daniel 3:18-21 KJV). Daniel was in a ravenous lions' den, in his hungry pit, but he came out and there weren't any teeth prints on him (Daniel 6:15-23 KJV).

You are entitled to a remarkable victory for your pain. Joseph had another son by the name of Ephraim, which means to be fruitful and abundant. God had made Joseph fruitful and abundant in the land. God blessed him tremendously with wealth and honor. God is not offended when you remind him of the victories we use in this book, after all it's in His word. God is waiting for you to declare your Manasseh and your Ephraim! He will give you your Ephraim. And your Manasseh will cause you to forget.

When Joseph's brothers realized who Joseph was they became afraid. They were afraid because of how evil they had been to him. Anything could have happened to him over the years. He could have died, and would have if they had their way. They were expecting Joseph to throw them into prison or even worse, execute them. Joseph did not react adversely to seeing them. Joseph now realized it was not their fault. The New Living Translation, of Genesis 45:5 says, "But don't be angry with yourselves that you did this to me, for God did it. He sent me here ahead of you to preserve your lives." And we know from studying this story that God did do it. He orchestrated the whole thing. It was all a part of God's plan for Joseph to go into that pit, and from a pit into a dungeon, and from the dungeon escape the sexual harassment of Mrs. Potiphar. Everything else that happened to Joseph was a part of God's plan.

Too many spouses blame each other for their marital problems, frustrated business partners blame the other for that failed business. It may be God's doing. Too many children blame their parents for not being able to go to college. It was probably God's doing. God may have wanted to give you a testimony. Remember without a test there is no testimony. Maybe He wanted to provide a platform to test your faith. Maybe He needed you to be dependent totally on him. Consider for a moment that God did it. He has a plan and a purpose for your life. Before you go on blaming other people for things that God may have done, think for a moment – could this be God's doing? God is the architect of the plans for our lives, it is good and not evil. The pain of the plan may feel immense. But there's no need to change the lyrics to the popular song from "Everything that has happened to me in my life – it was God" to - Everything that has happened to me that was good- it was God. It's all good…because it's all God.

Only mature Christians know that God does not only orchestrate things for us that feel good, he's the master of plans and knows the ending before it happens. So go ahead and sing the song the way it was written and pay homage to a God that knows what 's good for you – even when the world says it is bad. He has already performed your ending before it even begins.

He gave Joseph incredible wisdom. His next feat of faith was the truest test of his love and forgiveness. How was he going to get his family back? He couldn't let them go back to his father right now. He knew he would never see them again. He loved them so much that he devised a scheme to get them back. He put money in one of the sacks of the brothers, and when the guards went after them they found the money in the sack. They were scared. The guards took them all back to the palace to Joseph. Joseph wanted to test them. He wanted to see if they had changed or if they were the same jealous, mean-spirited attempted murderers. They had previously told him that they had a younger brother that had been left home with their father. Joseph asked them to bring their younger brother. If they did they would be spared.

They refused to bring Benjamin because they knew it would break Jacob's heart. He had already lost one son and wasn't about to loose another. The brothers began to offer themselves to Joseph instead of their brother Benjamin. This showed Joseph that they had finally learned what sacrifice was all about, but he did not relent. He wanted to see his brother and eventually wanted his family in Egypt with him. So the brothers agreed to bring Benjamin back and Joseph kept Simeon in Egypt to ensure the brothers' return. The brothers did indeed bring Benjamin back and Joseph cried once again because he would be with his blood brother again. They both had the same mother and father. Jacob and the rest of the family, 80 people in total, moved to Egypt to be with Joseph and escaped the famine.

When you look at where Joseph started out, and where he ended up, you can see that where you come from does not prescribe where you will end up. Your beginnings may be saddled with pitfalls from an impoverished heritage. But you can end up with the riches and righteousness God preordained for you.

Joseph went into more than one pit. God brought Joseph out of every one of them and brought him to honor and majesty. God will do the same thing for you when you profess the I AM that you truly are, as opposed to what the world says you are. You don't have to be a rocket scientist or have a degree in physics to see that the shortest distance between two points is a straight line.

The distance between your beginning and your ending may seem far reaching or even unattainable. In your most desperate and hopeless position, as a follower of Christ, you are still on the path of that impenetrable straight line - the word of God. Stay on course, as Joseph did, because where you are right now is not going to matter when you come out of your pit.

Chapter Two

YOU ARE RICHER THAN SOLOMON

*N*ot until our so-called modern day society did we begin this notion that wealth doesn't belong to the people of God. This is something new. The very reason there was such reluctance to accept Jesus as the Messiah - was because the wealth centered generation of that time wanted a messiah born into royalty, one that reeked of wealth and privilege. Even the poorest of the poor didn't want to embrace a savior that was born homeless, raised by a carpenter that hung out with low-lifes. They wanted a rich redeemer and nothing less. Had they but heeded the prophets, they would have known of Him what He was, the very definition of wealth, the epitome of affluence clothed in humility by His father.

Even though they didn't pass the test of His father's disguise – they at least expected the appearance of wealth.

Only in a day like ours do we allow such faulty thinking that suggests a man or woman of the cloth live by paltry means. Such thinking would never have been tolerated In the Bible days. Nothing short of physical punishment would be the penalty for anyone questioning the wealth of the Ecclesiasts of that time. Today, it has become common place for worthy disciples to have to defend their wealth against rumors of compromised gain.

Wealthy and righteous men didn't just start with the mega television ministries of today. I'd like to say that the wealthy and righteous people of today are using the template from those of yesterday. The Bible has always had a lot of rich people in it. There was Abraham. He was extremely rich. He owned tons of livestock, which is like saying today that he owned most of the shares in Microsoft. Then there was Job. He was the very definition of rich and righteous. He owned boo coo shares in Microsoft. King David was pretty rich himself, but these men were not only rich men. They were also holy men. Abraham was called a righteous man of God. Job was called a perfect man (Job 1:1 KJV). And David was a man after God's own heart.

These are fine examples of holy, rich men, but we can't go further without mentioning the richest of them all. Most of us are familiar with the story of King Solomon, in I Kings 3:5-13 KJV. King Solomon was God's chosen heir to King David's (his father) throne. He became the wisest, richest and most influential king in Israel's history. Shortly after King Solomon's appointment God appeared to him in a vision, asking him what he wanted.

I shutter to think what will happen If God came to any one of us today and asked us that question. At the top of that list, and it would have been a list - not just one thing; we would invariably say in the infamous words of that Oscar winning actor, "Show me the money!" King Solomon being the man of God that he was asked God for an obedient heart and the understanding of right and wrong so that he could rule the people well. Because King Solomon did not act selfishly God not only granted him wisdom and understanding He also blessed him with wealth and honor. King Solomon is known in the Bible as the richest and wisest man to ever live. What a way to go down in history!

The Bible says that King Solomon's wisdom could not be measured. That's how smart he was. King Solomon wrote over 3,000 proverbs and 1,000 songs. Many people came from great distances to hear his wisdom. He had an extensive knowledge about of plant life, fish, birds, animals and insects. In addition to that, his great wisdom has made us all marvel at one time or another, particularly the story of the two women that brought the baby before King Solomon, which, of course was a tremendous display of King Solomon's wisdom.

Aside from him having an IQ that was off the meter, King Solomon was also very rich. His kingdom stretched from the Euphrates River to Egypt, which is a pretty vast distance. King Solomon was the king responsible for building the first temple in Israel, which was not just any temple. King Solomon's temple was over 20 stories high which was an unfathomable feat for three thousand years ago. There was a special room for the Ark of the Covenant called the Holy of Holies and this room was covered in 600 tons of pure gold.

In this temple even the floors were covered in gold. While King Solomon was building the temple he was also building his palace. Only divine wisdom could make you that daring, It was built from Cedar (which was an expensive commodity) and constructed from hand crafted blocks of stone. Bronze pillars also supported the structure. Can you imagine how much this palace would cost to build if King Solomon was around today? Now that is truly living the lifestyle of the rich and the righteous.

It goes without saying that King Solomon was a very, very rich man, but unlike the celebrities of the famed TV show he was also a man of God. He had a relationship with God and a pure heart. He was obedient and humble, and this is why God blessed him. King Solomon was able to create a definitive balance in areas of his life that most of us do not exercise today. This is the very thing that sparks fear in the minds of many Christians. Because of the imbalance often taught or, left out in our teaching of Biblical truths, many fear aspiring towards financial prosperity with the same zeal as their spiritual prosperity.

The Bible doesn't tell us not to seek prosperity at all, it simply instructs us not to seek it first. In the third epistle to John 2:2 the Apostle Paul expressed prosperity as his most earnest desire for the church. Yet, Sunday after Sunday in pulpits across this country the imbalance is enthusiastically preached. The word of God remains perfectly balanced, leaving no room for doubt if we only dare to strive for the revelation of scripture as opposed to a mere Sunday sermon.

The Controversy

So if King Solomon was so rich and so wise how can we be greater or richer than he was? I Kings 3:13 says that there would never be another in his day as great as King Solomon. If that is so, then the title of this chapter would be a contradiction to the Bible. The statement that we are greater than King Solomon has certainly had its share of controversy. But richer than King Solomon too– how dare we? Yet the Word of God has no holes, it is airtight and flawless, and one scripture would never contradict another. In Matthew 12:42 it says, "The Queen of the South will rise at the judgment with this generation and condemn it; for she came from the ends of the earth to listen to Solomon's wisdom, and now one greater than Solomon is here." Jesus is the one that is greater than King Solomon.

I remember first getting this revelation from God about ten years ago. I courageously mounted the pulpit and preached "You Are Greater Than Solomon". Shortly after the sermon a minister approached me. I could see her discomfort with my sermon a mile away. She, being committed to her denominational teaching reminded me that there would never be anyone greater than King Solomon. In essence, what she was saying was that there is no way that *she* could possibly see *herself* as greater than King Solomon.

Without true revelation of the Holy Word we cannot see ourselves as ever being true conquerors, let alone more than conquerors. Many people may agree with my well-meaning friend. They may feel uncomfortable with any liberating revelation because bondage has a way of taking hostages.

The Word of God is the only thing that can truly make you free. When Jesus made the statement one is here that is greater than Solomon, He was audaciously talking about Himself. As the one that is greater, (He was richer too) He was the fulfillment of prophecy. Chapter 3, verse 13 says "there would never be one greater than Solomon in "his day". King Solomon's day has passed. Jesus' birth ushered in a new day; therefore, a greater one than King Solomon was on the scene. We know that 1 John 4:4 says, "greater is He that is in you, than he that is in the world." Greater is He that is within you and He that is within you is greater than King Solomon.

In effect, because Christ is in you, you are greater than King Solomon was. However, the controversy is not as much about our greatness versus King Solomon's, as much as it is about our wealth being greater than King Solomon's wealth. That's the thing that people have a problem with – because to be proven, means we have to put up. People don't have a problem dealing with the greatness so much, because greatness can be relative or abstract. The problem they have is: "if I'm richer than King Solomon, then where is my money"? The answer is where was Jesus' wealth when He made that statement? In heaven (with His Father) destined to be manifested on this earth, just as yours and mine is.

There is no reflection on you or I if we don't have the tangible manifestation of riches and wealth at the time you proclaim the Word. The Word of God is our unfailing foundation – we must declare what Jesus declared! God wants us to operate on the same principle that He uses – and that is that He spoke every miracle and every order of creation into existence before it actually materialized in this earth. So there is no so called burden of proof on you or I, for emulating our Father. Furthermore, the success of the Word of God does not depend on you, it has already been proven and finished.

It's funny that we don't allow ourselves to be trapped into that kind of dense thinking when it comes to our salvation. Whether our critics see the signs of transformation in us matters nothing at all to us. Despite their doubt of our conversion we continue to confess our redemption confidently. He wants us to be just as confident in every belief.

Some people actually think Jesus didn't mean wealth when He made that declaration of superiority. Don't think for one minute that Jesus was excluding wealth or riches when he declared Himself as being greater than Solomon.

He was being inclusive and not exclusive when He said I am greater. He meant I am richer too. Our Lord came from Heaven where the greatness, the treasure, and ultimate riches of His Father is. He was just here on a mission to save the world that would entitle us to the very same riches. He didn't exclude an ounce of His wealth when he referred to being greater than Solomon. He wasn't leaving it up to us to draw our own conclusion about the total essence of greatness. Although it appears that that is what many of us think.

I'm happy that you don't have to rely on me for the truth I'm committed to showing you in the scriptures so that this truth isn't based on my opinion. This is the unfailing Word of God, it is as unfailing as salvation. And if that's not enough to convince you, Jesus in another passage compared us to King Solomon again. In

Luke 12:27 (KJV) Jesus said, "Consider the lilies how they grow: they toil not, they spin not; and yet I say unto you, that Solomon in all his glory was not arrayed like one of these." Consider the lilies and how they are adorned.

They are more dressed up than King Solomon was in his finest robes. If He did that for the lilies what about you? Would he not want more for you than for lilies? God wants you to be better off than flowers, which (according to the scripture) are even better off than King Solomon. In verse 30, our Lord is saying not to worry about the daily cares of our lives as unbelievers do (the NLT says it dominates their thoughts), our lives are taken care of by virtue of our acceptance to this lifestyle which He encourages can be richer than Solomon's. Does that sound like a God that doesn't want you to have wealth? He wouldn't have chosen to illustrate His meaning by using a man that personified wisdom and wealth – to say I will do greater for you than the lilies which I have already provided for greater than Solomon. He was illustrating what you and I already have. He then continues with the warning for us to not let it dominate our thoughts He doesn't want us to emulate the mindset of heathens – so don't let it dominate your thoughts!

Careful, to do so would mean to be as the heathens. As far as the cares of this life goes – anything you care about – God has taken care of. Furthermore, contrary to popular opinion, our Father is not a repo man. God gets no pleasure in your car being repossessed or your home being foreclosed. And perish the thought that He doesn't want you to ever own a home or possess a car.

Here's another big news flash for your spirit. You could never own too many earthly possessions for God. It's all His anyway, which makes it jointly ours. It gives God immense pleasure for us to own multiple cars and multiple homes whether you ever cut a record, write a book or appear on TV, you are eligible and entitled because you are His!

Everything that God has is ours, and everything in the world is God's. We are joint heirs to His possessions because of Jesus Christ. Joint means that we have the same privileges as Jesus. It is the same concept of a joint bank account. The two names on the account both have access to everything in the account. One does not need the others permission to withdraw or deposit funds. As joint heirs we are entitled to all that is Jesus'.

Even when Jesus was on earth he did not bask in poverty. Jesus called to follow Him men that were entrepreneurs and he put them on His payroll. Jesus had a treasury and a treasurer (Judas Iscariot). I don't know any poor people with treasurers. Jesus' robe was of the finest quality. It didn't even have a seam in it. It was so valuable that the soldiers at His crucifixion gambled over His robe. Jesus lived abundantly on earth and so should we.

People like that minister I mentioned before get self righteous when you dare to speak about desiring luxury. They actually fight for the right to be broke. Their belief is actually born out of the teaching that to live in luxury or to desire luxury is prideful and has no place in the church, but this is hypocritical of them because they honestly do want luxury for themselves. They admire luxury. Instead of harnessing honest aspirations towards gaining it, which would be aligned with the Word of God, they too often, resent other people's possessions or pass judgment on others because of their wealth, which is an absolute sin. The greatest truth about wealth, prosperity and luxury is not a mystery. It has always been God's will for us to prosper. The Bible is chock full of these truths from Genesis to Revelation, as much is said in the Bible about wealth and luxury as sin and salvation.

The Four Things That King Solomon Did Not Know

The fact that Jesus said that a greater one than Solomon is on the scene is not the only evidence that proves that we are greater than Solomon.

Solomon himself admitted that he did not know everything, and some of the things that he admitted to not knowing separate him from us and the knowledge and wisdom that we now have.

King Solomon in all his wisdom and wealth was smart enough to admit that he had limitations. In Proverbs chapter thirty verses one through four (Pr 30:1-4) King Solomon speaks of some of the things he does not understand. These things separate us (those who are living by faith through grace) from King Solomon who lived by the law. This also illustrates another reason why we are truly greater than King Solomon. These four points are symbolic representations of the Body of Christ, the church. King Solomon had some insight of the things that would come, but, though, he could see these things - he could not understand them. Operating solely under the law you can never completely understand God's Grace.

Grace has an inconceivable redeeming value. It enables us to withstand and overcome seemingly impossible odds. There is no question that King Solomon had faith in God - he knew God and had great respect for his father King David. Solomon exercised as much or more faith as anyone could under the law. However, the law cannot make enough allowances for things only to be comprehended through grace.

The Eagles

Proverbs 30: 18-19, "There be three things which are too wonderful for me, yea, four which I know not: The way of the eagle in the air". King Solomon does not understand how the eagles can soar up, and swoop down, remain in the air and is still able to land solidly and safely every time. This statement or example draws an analogy of the similarity of the eagles and the church. The eagles are symbolic of the church, the body of Christ. It signifies the ups and downs that we, individual members of the body, and even the body as a whole go through. Still, despite these ups and downs, swoops and loops we are able to remain in the air indefinitely and land on our feet. King Solomon was amazed by this.

It is only because of the dispensation of God's Grace that we are troubled on every side yet *not* distressed. Grace allows us to, although winded and weak land on our feet and get back up with the wings of an eagle and fly again. Solomon had not experienced the recovering powers of Grace and was baffled by this.

The Ship

The second thing that amazed the King is "The way of a ship in the midst of the sea". King Solomon could not understand how a ship goes out to sea, encounters a storm and is able to find its way back home. Living in an era before maps, cartographers, and when folks still thought the world was flat the sea and sailing were a great mystery. King Solomon did not understand that the greatest captain of all navigates the SS Body of Christ. With Him at the helm it is easy to find your way back. It does not matter what meets you out there on the sea.

Whether it be waves or whales, the children of Grace know that conquering the sea is not dependant on the ship but the captain – it may sound cliché but if Jesus is truly your captain and not the co-Captain, even if it means walking the water our Lord has come through before and will again. The Holy Spirit (Christ in us) is our inner compass which gives us all the lighting we need to direct us. John 14:26 (NIV) " But the Counselor, the Holy Spirit, whom the Father will send in my name, will teach you all things. Jesus was saying I am sending you a comforter, a helper, an instructor, a guide and I give you a peace that surpasses the world's understanding that you do not have to worry or ever be afraid – no matter what you're facing.

How could the great King Solomon possibly know this experience? The Body of Christ represents the ship that has been tossed by the waves of time since the inception of the early church. We've been kicked around and we are perplexed, as the Apostle Paul taught, but *not* in despair and we always find our way back.

The Maiden

Proverbs 30:19 King Solomon has conflict about something else he does not understand. "The way of a man with a maid". King Solomon, named as the Romeo of his day could not understand how a man could only love one woman. For a man who had as many wives and concubines as he did this was inconceivable. His mind could not begin to conceive the one-woman man concept. It's too bad that King Solomon lived almost three thousand years before Percy Sledge said "When a man loves a woman she can't do nothing wrong."

King Solomon was living in a time when it was accepted or at least tolerable to have many wives. It was certainly acceptable to have multiple "sweethearts". Thank God we live in a different time now. When we stand before that man or woman of God we pledge ourselves to that other person 'til death do us part. We are bone of one's bone, flesh of one's flesh, and the two become one. King Solomon could not become one with anybody, not even (Pharaoh's daughter) his true heart's desire. There was not enough of him to go around. 1 Kings 11:3 KJV tells us that the good King had 700 wives and 300 concubines.

He did not understand nor could he appreciate the love of just one woman. There was no such thing as boy meets girl, that nervous first date, courtship, or even engagements for that matter – who has time for all of that - certainly not the good King.

Though he was rich enough to buy his way into the hearts of women, there was no way he could experience true love with any one of them. William Wordsworth wrote "Nothing can bring back the hour of the splendor in the grass and the glory of the flower." I think His Highness never wasted time with just one woman. Who has an hour when you have 1000 women telling you to take out the trash? His majesty is recognized as the world's greatest romantic, being credited for the writings of the sensual Songs Of Solomon of the Old Testament. Yet the honorable King remains baffled by – how to love just one woman. In fairness to King Solomon's plight we can't be too hard on him when it comes to the wondrous union of marriage. Even the Apostle Paul said it was a great mystery Ephesians 5:31-32.

The mystery of marriage also symbolizes the ultimate union or relationship. This is the relationship between Christ and the church. Jesus referred to Himself as the groom and the church as His bride. The love a husband has for his wife and the role of the husband should mirror the love Jesus has for us and the role He plays in our lives. Loving one woman so much that you would give your life (Ephesians 5:25) for her was beyond King Solomon's comprehension.

What a risk it would be for a man of the King's caliber to put all of his eggs in one basket and forfeit the comfort zone of knowing that no less than a thousand women have your back. Just think of the humility it would take to put another's needs before your own, for once, to forsake all others, to cleave only to the trust of one, exposing your faults and vulnerabilities, your loyalty and your nakedness to only that person, understanding that when she hurts, you hurt, when she cries, you cry, when she's broke, you're broke, when she's persecuted, you're persecuted, but *not* forsaken – until death do you part. No, King Solomon, living in the setting of his time could never understand that.

The Serpent

The final thing that perplexed the King is "the way of a serpent upon a rock". King Solomon could not fathom how the serpent crawls upon a rock, appearing to have no grip and is able to maintain its balance. In fact the serpent crawls from one extremity of the rock to another never revealing the source of its skillfulness. The serpent, appearing to become one with the rock envelopes itself beneath the rock when the threat of a predator emerges. How this could be astonished the wise king.

We know that the rock represents Jesus Christ. He is the rock on which the Body of Christ stands. It may look to the world as if our footing is not sure. The world can't see the power of the word deposited in us, making it appear as if our foundation is hopeless. Living in a world that relies on the surety of natural senses – it's foolish to hang on to mere faith when everything around you is falling. The natural mind tells us to do something that makes sense, something that we can see and feel to pacify our need to believe we are in control. Just as the serpent's ability to adhere to a rock is within – so is our ability to hold on. The power of the Word deposited in us is invisible.

The world can't see how the Word of God literally holds us fast to the Rock that is Jesus; making it impossible to fall. King Solomon's curiosity of the serpent on the rock is comparable to the curiosity of people today. How, if the surface of the rock is uneven does the serpent negotiate the edge of the rock? Why, if the rock's surface is rough does the serpent find comfort in its foundation? Similarly, why does a person choose a life surrendered to Jesus, the foundation though sure, is rough and unyielding, testing the faith of those that dare trust in Him. The only reasonable answer to "why" is found in the Apostle Paul's greatest work, his letter to the Romans. Romans 8:18 "For I reckon that the sufferings of this present time are not worthy to be compared with the glory which shall be revealed in us.

While our faith is being tested, it is also being fueled by the promise of glory. Only those who endure have the hope of realizing the glory in the end. Without a doubt, one day in the future our God will reveal who His children really are. This is why we hang on to the rock. For the glory…we do it for the glory. The Believer, as the serpent, moves effortlessly around the rock without falling. It must appear to the unbeliever, as if we may fall at any moment, alas the survival of the serpent - as the Christian is not dependant on themselves, but the rock. Certainly part of our testing is also the recovery. And the varying degrees of scars from of the battle reveal that we're still in the fight. That truth keeps us faithfully depending on the rock, and though we may be cast down, we are *not* destroyed.

Is there any wonder why King Solomon couldn't understand the mystery of Grace? It doesn't surprise me at all that a man that could righteously decide life or death in a split second, blessed with unsurpassed wisdom - couldn't understand these four seemingly small things. God, who possesses the ultimate wisdom allowed Solomon to ponder these things so that we, being wiser (with the Holy Spirit) could answer the mysteries of how the peaks and valleys of life could be no match for the wings of an eagle, and how understanding a woman is in the beauty of oneness, only learned through fidelity, or how the foundation that is the rock holds sure against any slippery surface, and, how the tossed ship battered and beaten, conquers the wind and the waves only to sail again another day.

What infinite wisdom our Father has, fulfilling the scripture with His church (The Body of Christ) as he that is greater than King Solomon. King Solomon was great. That is in indisputable. He had a brilliant mind, beautiful women and a treasure chest of riches, yet the things he could not understand are more valuable than the things that he did understand. In actuality, we are probably not a fraction as brilliant as King Solomon was, but our access to Grace and the wisdom of God can bring us greater spiritual and material wealth than King Solomon.

Are we not blessed to be living in the dispensation of Grace? Where would we be if it were not for Grace? King Solomon undoubtedly had great wisdom and possessed great wealth, yet he experienced the great void that could only have been filled through knowing Grace. Had King Solomon known of such Grace, he being full of wisdom would have instantly traded all of his riches to live under Grace. God's Grace will add to you what money and possessions never could.

How Far Are You Willing To Go?

In I Kings chapter ten the Queen of Sheba has come to visit King Solomon. The knowledge of his wisdom and wealth has spread across the region like a wildfire. King Solomon was something of a phenomenon in his day. People were in awe of him. He was to them what Albert Einstein is to our era. The King was an ambassador of peace and ahead of his time in accomplishments. If His Majesty were alive today he would undoubtedly be recipient of the coveted Nobel Peace Prize. King Solomon had a beautiful mind.

The Queen heard about the King's beautiful mind and the things he had done. She heard about his infinite wisdom and how he administered judgment. Seduced by what she had heard and intrigued at the possibility of one as rich, or richer than herself, she prepared for an arduous expedition. The queen, (called Mekeda as a child) is recorded as being of extremely beautiful appearance; (with the exception of reports of a depilatory leg, foot or ankle) she was gracious and skillfully intelligent. She was also an eloquent speaker, noted for her gift of diplomacy and excellence in public relations. The qualities she possessed were not unlike those she'd heard Solomon possessed. Yet her quest for greater wisdom would be the driving force behind her journey. The exploration would roughly take 3000 miles roundtrip in the Arabian Desert.

She would be accompanied by thousands of Sheba-ettes (guards servants and handmaidens) and accordingly about 800 camels, mules and donkeys. With great anticipation, the young virtuous queen sets off. Such a journey would require at least six months due to the consideration needed for camels - being able to only travel about 20 miles per day. She must have had reservations about the trip but her quest for truth outweighed any fears she may have had. Sheba's caravan was laden with precious gifts and treasures for the King. Among her provisions of vast wealth included the costly gold, frankincense and myrrh the very offerings that would later foreshadow the arrival of THE King – Jesus.

Her Excellency traveled northward through the dessert in the scorching sun to get to King Solomon. Her goal was to see if his reputation and good name would pass the test of her hard questions. King Solomon's name brought great honor to the name of the Lord and the queen wanted to experience the essence of it. Braving harsh desert conditions was a small price to pay for what she hoped to gain. The queen was more than willing to go the extra mile. She needed to know how he acquired such great wealth and wisdom, whether it was from his God as he claimed it was, even if it meant coming to know his God, even that distance was not too far for her.

When she got there and saw everything that she had heard about, her breath was taken away. What she had heard was true, yet this was beyond her expectations. She was astonished by the lavish and elegant spread of feasts - Martha Stewart and Betty Crocker put together couldn't pull off a smorgasbord like this. This was beyond her wildest imagination, his attendants, arrayed like soldiers, the servants clothes alone screamed luxury. His valets had valets. Every guest's cup refilled before it was empty. What organization, what structure - what a king! If that wasn't enough to move her, his palace certainly did. There's not a woman alive that wouldn't be impressed by a crib like the King's. Solomon's digs took him thirteen years to complete and it showed, his living quarters over 75 feet long, surrounded a beautiful courtyard.

The architecture was precise down to every intricate detail, not a corner of the palace was overlooked. More incredible, was his attention to symbolic detail.

Solomon erected six foot tall bronze lilies that sat atop 27 foot tall pillars. No coincidence here at all. The great wise King was prophetically portraying the beautiful revelation of Jesus in Matthew 6:28-29. The Queen was not only wowed by Solomon, but Solomon's God knocked her socks off too. She was astounded at how King Solomon could have all that he had because of his God of Israel. Her God of the sun and the moon and all the other elements never influenced her to righteousness. Check out what she says in verse 9 NLT: *"The Lord your God is great indeed! He delights in you and has placed you on the throne of Israel. Because the Lord loves Israel with an eternal love, He has made you king so you can rule with justice and righteousness."* The Queen has come under repentance!

This is clear cut evidence of what will happen when you go the extra mile. There is nothing to be gained by sitting back and criticizing or speculating about the truth, dying in unbelief, and being doubtful of the miraculous. Yes, the miraculous, because this was truly miraculous. She was so moved that she came under repentance and she didn't just stop there. She gave King Solomon spices that surpassed Biblical proportions. Verse 10 NLT describes the quantity as being the largest cargo of spices ever. Her gain and Solomon's gain was all because someone was not afraid to go above and beyond the ordinary.

Disregard the doubters, the fearful and the unbelievers that stand on the sidelines of faith for the prevention of the supernatural.

Perhaps the good Queen under estimated her own wisdom. It could only be divine wisdom to inspire someone to travel that distance to see a man of above-human magnitude and leave him with gifts making him not only richer than you – but much richer than he already was – only supernatural wisdom could have driven her. The queen was out to prove that she could make a statement adding to his already incomprehensible wealth. Can you imagine being so moved (or converted) that you leave *your* greatest wealth to the wealthiest man alive? Sheba unloaded nine thousand pounds of gold to the already well-to-do king. It mattered very little or nothing at all that he was already richer than her. Her royal highness, just like everyone of us was searching for the truth. She left King Solomon a whole lot richer than when she came.

This is because he imparted wisdom to her. Proverbs (one of Solomon's greatest works) advises us that wisdom is far more precious than the price of gold, rubies or pearls, and nothing you can desire can be compared to wisdom Pr. 3:13-14.

The Queen of Sheba gained more than she gave, because she was willing to go the extra mile. The extra mile is what Gospel recording artist Donnie McClurkin was singing about in the song Stand. Even if that something extra is just standing, even if it is just holding on to what little faith you have left. That may be the extra mile required of you. But how far are you willing to go? What are you willing to leave behind to live the lifestyle that's balanced in spiritual as well as naturally? Are you willing to travel across a dessert of disbelief? Are you willing to seek divine wisdom? Or are you going to take some other path knowing that only God's truth is the key?

Are you waiting on a push like the Queen? Makeda didn't realize what her full potential was until it was put to the test. Everything she did is identified as the search for truth. When you earnestly seek for truth, you will find it. She sought for a truth more real than she had known and a righteousness she had never known. A contradictory legend depicts the young queen making the trek to become romantically involved with the handsome young King. The Bible gives no account of that; little more is said Biblically about their time together. It is possible that they found more than a platonic interest in each other during her stay. Verse 13 NLT only says "King Solomon gave the queen of Sheba whatever she asked for, besides all the customary gifts he had so generously given."

It's tempting not to entertain the thought of a passionate romance and future love child born to the beautiful couple. Nevertheless, the Biblical truth is an even juicier story. Verse 6 and 7 gives the true account of exactly why her majesty took the exhausting voyage. "Everything I heard in my country about your achievements and wisdom is true! I didn't believe it until I arrived here and saw it with my own eyes." There's no getting around it the truth must be experienced! It wasn't enough for her to hear the truth from reliable sources (and she had many). She could have saved a bundle by sending her own sources to King Solomon to bring back a report with tangible evidence of his existence. She was driven by a force that pushed her into a will that was not her own. It was the competitiveness of her royal breeding that fueled her conquest.

God knows how to stimulate our desires. He knows what it takes to get us into the center of His will, and it may be through sheer competition. A little competitive edge won't hurt you. It forces you to get better. What queen worth her weight in gold - wouldn't saddle up a few camels to go and see a wise man that could change her life? If true, she was destined to get answers for her life and her country that her father before her couldn't have. The mere thought of you being sized up against another peer forces you to bring your "A" game. Just look at professional sports. Do you think that if they were playing just for fun they would be so good? Competition is a tremendous motivational force. It forces you to excel, or, if nothing else at least find your potential. The desire to be better pushes you to do just that – get better at giving more and invariably you'll receive more.

Competition Rocks!

When I was younger and my husband first started showing interest in me, I refused to show my hand to him. I didn't want him to know that I was just as interested. As young women we are taught to use this strategy as an advantage over men. I knew I had him based on his reaction to my disinterest. Then a new girl moved into our neighborhood. She was beautiful with long hair and a shapely figure. Well, my husband, then just a friend, started to show interest in this girl, and she (obviously not taught by the same school I was) began returning his interest. What was happening here? Something went wrong somewhere. I abandoned my so-called strategy. I had to get myself together before it was too late. I started dressing up. I got my hair done and began returning his kindnesses. But it wasn't until I had some competition that I got on the ball. I hated to admit It, but I was jealous!

The Bible makes a great case for the fact that there is an incredible force at work when someone forfeits or stumbles at their opportunity. It may be best described as the spirit of competition. Because we just don't want to call it plain ole jealousy. But we must remember that God called it jealousy. He chose the Gentiles to make the Jews jealous. Romans 11:11-12 NLT asks specifically, *"Did God's people stumble and fall beyond recovery? Of course not! His purpose was to make His salvation available to the Gentiles, and then the Jews would be jealous and want it for themselves."* His purpose, yes- -it was His purpose to do this? This means God intentionally used an evil force to get His desired end.

God knows how we process thought as well as what motivates us. He knew that just a presentation of the truth alone would not be stirring enough to convert the Jews. He also knew that their nature was to be arrogant, self-assured and impressed with their own goodness. You know, already saved.

This was the same false confidence that plagued me, until presented with the jealousy brought on by another woman. It forced me to convert. God did the only divine thing that could be done to get the Jews to convert. He threw some competition at them to provoke them to jealousy as a plan to get them to serve Him and to bless them. The Apostle Paul says in verse 12, *"Now if the Gentiles were enriched because the Jews turned down God's offer of salvation, think how much greater a blessing the world will share when the Jews finally accept it."* (when we reach God's desired end) Apostle Paul was teaching us that there is still something greater that we should expect because of this awesome plan of salvation.

The first thing is found in verse 11: - that those who do accept salvation are enriched. He was not referring to being enriched in the great by-and-by some day in heaven.

God wants so much for us to be enriched on this earth that he devised an elaborate yet simple plan to impact our condition while on earth. The plan is called salvation. In addition to guaranteeing us eternal life with Him in heaven, He was also conveying that we shall have riches and wealth on earth now. He was specifically making known the truth about "earthly wealth" that comes as a byproduct of salvation.

The KJV actually uses the term *"riches"* from the Greek word *ploutos* taken from the root, *ploutizo* literally meaning wealthy, or to make rich - to have money, possessions, abundance and riches.

It's crystal clear, salvation brings riches! And riches come from salvation! And by accepting Jesus, the state of *ploutos,* (wealth and riches) should be happening to every one of us! The only thing that separates us from wealth is our willingness to go the extra mile. How far we are willing to go to believe the seldom accepted truth of God's word. By now you know that the extra mile is not a physical journey, but a spiritual one. It is a journey that occurs in the corners of one's mind. It is the determination to go above and beyond the obstacles that wage war against faith.

I said earlier in the book that we were dealing with balance. The balance of God's plan is unmistakable. Salvation and riches in exchange for sin and death. Why would anyone fight this plan? Yet many Christians do – when you fight prosperity, you are fighting God's plan, and inadvertently living beneath your privilege.

As I've previously shown you, God does not get any glory from you suffering lack - particularly because He has made provision for you to have wealth through His plan of salvation. But there is still even more.

The second and most incredible thing is this: what happens now is even greater than acquiring wealth and riches. The other incredible occurrence of salvation is that the world is affected by it. You say - how could someone accepting Christ change the world? Verse 12 NLT says that this is a "much greater blessing".

When people finally accept Jesus as God's substitute for their sin, the entire world around them shares in their blessing, and this is greater.

Let's look at the word *"world"* in the scripture. In the Greek translation, the word world is *"kosmos"* the word used by Paul, which means the universe in an orderly sense or arrangement. God purposed it to be so, that when you accept His Son, which is His plan – your life will inevitably take on a divine order and arrangement. Your former cursed order and arrangement takes on the change that only salvation can bring. At first it may not feel like it's a greater blessing, yet every bit of chaotic disorder has now come subject to your confession and is doomed to failure.

The disconnection with old friends and even close relatives may appear to be the disorder but in effect it is the result of the new order, and arrangement of your world now in Christ. This may just be temporary until your new order begins to affect theirs. I would love to promise you that it is, but I can't because it may even get worse. You should rest in knowing that this is all part of God's divine plan for your new life, and that your savior Jesus Christ is also your comforter through the pain of this incredible change.

By the way, it is no coincidence that *kosmos is* the same word used in the Greek in the Gospel of Mark by Jesus Christ in chapter 16, verse 15.

Jesus makes an indisputable final statement before His ascension to heaven. He said – "Go ye into all the world or *"kosmos"*, and preach the Gospel to every creature." And if that wasn't enough, he goes on to give confirmation to what Paul teaches in Romans. In verse 16 He explains what the impact of preaching the Gospel does. "He that believes and is baptized will be saved. But he that believeth not shall be damned." Our Lord wanted to make a tremendous impact here and He did! Jesus was saying that only the Gospel can reverse damnation – and change the world. Jesus wanted us to understand that there are definite consequences to preaching the true saving Gospel. People will believe, and they will be saved. And consequently, when they don't believe, they will be condemned.

Notice that Jesus didn't leave room for any gray area. By hearing the Gospel: You will either be saved or be damned! Notice that He wasn't concerned with the what ifs…what if they are this - or what if they are that – the only thing that matters is what is. The saved and the damned is all there is. There is no such category for the undecided, the ignorant, the poor, or the waiting to be judged. Jesus was about to leave His friends and followers – and He couldn't waste precious words trying to cover every imaginable state of man's mind. He knew there is only one state before you accept Jesus – lost. A master of discerning the condition of our hearts, Jesus staged it so that regardless of who you are, where you are, your religion, or any other factors, you will either believe and be saved, or not believe - and be damned.

Preaching the Gospel instantaneously assigns an order and ar-rangement to the hearer. It's automatic, the power of the Gospel purposely assigns us residence into one of the two categories – saved or damned. Nothing else known to man can do that.

Isn't that a "greater" condition as Paul states in Romans 11:12, to be able to change the *"kosmos"* or world through faith? We are able to change the order and arrangement of our lives and others when we, the believer use the infallible Gospel. It will convert or condemn.

Let's review this revelation: Jesus Christ taught in Mark 16:15 & 16 "Go into the kosmos and preach the Gospel to every creature, and its supernatural power will reverse the order and arrangement of damnation in the entire universe".

The Apostle Paul taught in Romans 11:11 & 12 "It was always God's plan for the Jews to reject Jesus initially; and become jealous because of the riches and wealth you receive - because you accepted Him instead." And by accepting him - you reverse your damnation, your original order and arrangement in the kosmos or universe."

Would God choose jealousy to set in motion His plan for salvation in the earth?

God could choose anything He wants to, and He knew it would take a force crueler than death to drive the Jews to repentance. The acquisition of wealth and riches of the Gentiles would be the only thing strong enough to provoke jealousy in the exalted hearts of His chosen people. The Bible teaches us that God's plans were often devised with the intention to confound, confuse and shut the mouths of the wise proud-hearted intellectuals. The Apostle Paul gives us this truth when he quotes the Prophet Isaiah in 1Corinthians chapter 1 and verse 19.

"For it is written, I will destroy the wisdom of the wise, and will bring to nothing the understanding of the prudent." The latter portion of verse 21 even says that God chose something as foolish as preaching to save us and reverse our damnation. **"it pleased God by the foolishness of preaching to save them that believe."** God even called preaching foolish, but He chose it.

It just doesn't make sense that God would promise us earthly wealth and riches as a result of accepting his Son Jesus as our savior. It sounds too far-fetched. This perhaps is the reason for such an imbalance in the preaching in our churches. They simply don't believe it.

We expect our spiritual state to change as a result of salvation, but we don't really expect our financial or fiscal state to change. The message of the cross is complete. It holds the key to your earthly state as well as your heavenly state. I'm not advocating that our preachers tell new believers to go out and get rich after repentance. Rather, that we as preachers remember that transformation of minds is critical in the process of conversion. New believers as all believers need a balanced Gospel preached to them. As preachers of the glorious Gospel of Christ, we are responsible as much for proclaiming the prosperity of the saving Gospel as much as we are responsible for preaching soul salvation.

The message shouldn't be that God doesn't want us to be rich it should be that, everything put in its right perspective, your soul should prosper even as your lifestyle prospers – or becomes rich. It was the most earnest desire in the Apostle John's teaching to Pastors in 3rd John 1:2 John states under divine influence that it is the utmost desire that we first have prosperity – wealth and riches, second, that we have physical wellness or perfect health, and third, that all of this happens at the same rate of our spiritual growth. This is what God wants for us. If this wasn't true God would not have allowed it to be in His book of facts – the Bible.

It is always ironic to me when those that believe in suffering the most resist it the most. If their belief is that all God wants from us is to bravely take on life's perils - why then do they fight for dear life for the suffering to let up? Shouldn't we want what God wants for us? I've said again and again that some of the most hurting people I know would suddenly spring back to their old selves again were they given a check for ten thousand dollars. A lot of the stress and mental anguish that we take as required suffering would be relieved with a prescription of a two-week vacation. All the martyrs suffering for the glory of God would make a bee line at the shameless offer of mere money to pay off those pesky bills.

Only a humorous view at this outrageous thinking can help salve the pain and sadness of the state of this belief system. People claim this to be in keeping with their standard of humility as required by God.

Poverty is not God's formula to keep us humble. The scripture reveals to us God's example of humility as being that of a child's heart. There's not a child that I know that can invent such a complicated misconception of the truth. In Matthew 18:2-4 KJV Jesus called a little child over to him and said to the disciples when asked who is the greatest in the kingdom of heaven. *"Verily I say unto you, except you be converted, and become as little children, ye shall not enter into the Kingdom of heaven. Whosoever therefore shall humble himself as this little child, the same is greatest in the kingdom of heaven."*

This scripture exemplifies humility 101. Living in poverty will not make you humble. Only the pureness and the innocence of the blood of Jesus can bring mankind back to the state of a child's heart. Some of the most proud people around are those that have nothing, and feel they are in some way more Holy or closer to God. Having no worldly possessions does not make you meek and lowly, nor does it make you the apple of God's eye. Poor people are not guaranteed to go to heaven and rich people are not guaranteed to go to hell. Jesus exclaimed in verse 3 that unless you are converted, (saved/born again) whether rich or poor your soul is eternally lost. Jesus expertly unmasked the disciples' proud hearts.

This is one of those exclusive places in scripture where He called for an immediate conversion by the believer himself. This change must happen now and must be done by your own will and desire to enter His Kingdom. Jesus didn't require of them to pray that humility would come, or even that fasting would destroy the haughty minded – no, he commanded that you, the owner of a prideful heart - humble your own self. Humility is its own reward – to humble yourself now means greatness in His kingdom.

The Faith that Acts Out

Without a doubt, this is not what you are hearing in most pulpits across the country. I can offer no apologies. The indisputable truth of the Word of God is not reflected by how popular it is or by how many preachers believe it. Your wealth is no more based on other people, than is your salvation. When God imparted His great truth into men by Holy inspiration it was not contingent on whether the masses believed it or not. Jesus nailed our poverty to the cross. He not only died for our sins, but He also died for our infirmities. He died to free us from any and every thing that may oppress us. There is no place in God's Holy Bible that requires us to live under any vow of poverty. But if you must – please, vow to fight poverty. Make a vow to reverse the error in the minds of God's people that insist on living without the pleasures God ordained for us to enjoy.

The God of all wisdom didn't reserve beauty, wealth and riches just for heaven. What would we have to compare it to – wouldn't we enjoy our heavenly mansion more, once we have had one on earth? Of course any earthly mansion would naturally pale in comparison to our heavenly one. You may not want a mansion on this earth, yet you are entitled to one. It is your entitlement to have earthly wealth as well as live holy. Just as certain as faith assures salvation, it also assures healing and a rich lifestyle while on earth. Yet, non-working faith is like a corpse, it is dead. And unfaithful works is also dead. Faith in God's word is not to just be admired or adored; it's not enough to feel good about having faith. God's word must be trusted as the vehicle which drives our actions.

The word of God does not become faith until it is propelled from the pages of the Bible and ignited by the fire of the faithful. Faith must be put into action! A favorite quote of mine is one by Ferdinand Foch – *"The most powerful weapon on earth is the human soul on fire."*

Faith in God is demonstrated by your actions - and your actions reveal how great your faith is.

Veronica, the woman in the Bible with a serious hemorrhage for twelve years had the faith that Jesus would heal her. She also took some extraordinary actions that revealed how great - her faith was. (Matthew 9:19-21 KJV). She knew that if she could just get to the mere fringe of His robe, it alone would make her whole. But what it would take for her to get to Jesus would be tantamount to climbing Mount Everest. Most folks could only demonstrate faith for their healing when they are touched. She knew within herself that this would never happen. For Him to touch her would mean making herself visible through the barrage of self-righteousness, cultural biases, and the classism of the Scribes and Pharisees, that beleaguered all commoners. She would also have to fight the prejudices of her time that relegated woman in her condition to hiding out. How dare she show herself in public, was their attitude. People, men especially, feared contamination of the likes of her. In the condition she was in, she was seen as no better than scum.

Her status as second class citizen not withstanding, she took action beyond it all. No longer hidden from her was the masters' popularity. The knowledge of His teachings had spread abroad. She wouldn't waste time with anything that would interfere with her mission. It was no longer rumor - the story she heard of Jesus forgiving the sins of a paralyzed man - at the initiative of his friends. She had also heard about the evil indictment of the religious leaders that scoffed at the miracle; accusing Jesus of blasphemy. But Jesus being forever a Master at upsetting the intolerance of fools – He baffled them and shut their mouths before they opened them. Responding to their condemnation, Jesus fired back - "Isn't it easier to say thy sins be forgiven thee than arise and walk?" Our fair lady knew about this. She also knew that no amount of physical labor to reach him would be harder to overcome - than bigotry like this. Nevertheless, her faith unfailing, she pressed through the crowd. Feeling assured that at the very least, the connection of her DNA against the supernatural fibers of His seamless robe - would undo her certain death. But at best, she would be miraculously and instantly made completely whole – not just freed from the disease that had so dominated her life, but also the sin that meant eternal ruin to her soul.

She didn't suffer from analysis paralysis like some of us, bogged down with information overload, making her too afraid to act. You can make journals from now till eternity and collect scriptures as if they're going out of style. But if you don't ever move in faith and put your faith in God to work – you will never see results.

Veronica was instantly and miraculously healed, saved and changed forever. The change was so incredible it seeped virtue form the savior's soul. Jesus knew He had been more than brushed up against. The act of her faith had forced him to take notice. He remarked that He felt the touch of her Faith. Veronica's story is the reason why many refuse to believe God for wealth; because it means taking serious action and changing old behaviors.

Something old…Something new

The story of the Shunammite woman in the Old Testament of II Kings 4:18-30 and the epistle of James 1:17 in the New Testament to the Jewish Christians makes another great case for the agreement of the scriptures. The Shunem woman proves that true faith inspires action while the Apostle James emphatically declares that faith unaccompanied by action is useless.

A woman of great resources, the Shunammite woman went against the obvious signs of nature that said assuredly her son was dead. At the first opportunity she had to call the situation exactly what it was - she refused. There was no doubt that her beloved son had expired. But her faith refused to say anything that didn't agree with the outcome she wanted. The first step in receiving what God's word says you can have is aligning your words with your faith.

It's pointless to pray for something and before you're done with the petition, you annihilate it with your words. Its finally time to let God off the hook for our so-called unanswered prayers that lay waste. God is not at fault because we didn't achieve our goals. His Holy word has been around this long because his mercy endures forever – and it may take that long for us to get the revelation.

You don't get what you want...you get what you believe! And consequently, you only say, that which you believe.

You will have what you say - so don't say anything you don't want to have.

Enterprising and successful – the Shunem woman knew how to get what she wanted. When asked by both Gehazi, Elisha's servant and the man of God himself - is everything alright, her misleading reply was "everything is fine." Every thing is fine...her son is dead and she claims everything is fine! She was either a remarkable liar, or she had remarkable faith. Perhaps she foreknew that to reveal the actual circumstances would predispose them to the hopelessness of the situation.

She wasn't about to take that chance. Her son was already dead – and in her mind the only event to follow death was burial. She didn't want that picture to be in their minds. Cleverly waiting for the moment when she could make personal contact with the prophet, she grabbed a hold of his leg and refused to let go until he she had his concurrence. The prophet concurred. The lad's healing was eminent. After all else had failed, the compassionate prophet wouldn't give up. He does the unthinkable, and positions himself atop the little man - and the weight of his anointing forces breath back into the boy's body. Seven sneezes later, the boy rushes back from heavens gates into the earthly realm.

Elisha knew that more than the fate of the boy was at hand. The faith of his friend was hinged on the boy's recovery. If that scenario had occurred today, the religious community wouldn't hesitate to rebuke her for her trickery and outright lie – overlooking the inevitable miracle that resulted. More times than I care to remember – some well-meaning clergy friend or acquaintance lovingly puts me in my place, whenever I deny my obvious aches and pains and profess that I'm healed. The appearance of possible dishonesty seems to be of greater concern to them than my prevailing faith. If the situation looks bleak – say it, if your body aches admit it, you're just being honest right? Where does honesty end and faith begin?

Don't condemn the faithful because they won't circum to the obvious hardships that tests their faith. Seven sneezes in a row may mean the beginnings of a cold to you - but to the faithful, it is the manifestation of the miraculous.

Her refusal to own up to the weight of her emotions was a test of faith. Her story teaches us that faith and works are married to each other. Faith must be integrated with works. There was never any doubt in her mind that Elisha could resuscitate her son. But she would need to turn a blind eye and a deaf ear to the enemies of her faith – the five senses. Faith must extend beyond what you can see hear and touch. Faith sees the invisible, hears the inaudible and believes the impossible – it transcends emotion and environmental limitations. Assuredly faith without works is dead – works without faith is dead, and so is your miracle without them both.

Chapter Three

HIS BUSINESS IS PLEASURE

*T*he modest-minded traditionalist might be hard pressed to believe that God is just as much in the business of pleasure as He is in the business of righteousness and judgment. The Gospel of Luke chapter 12, verse 32 reveals a shinning example of how passionate the Father is about pleasure. He not only wants it for His children, He Himself fervently gleans pleasure from us. Jesus explains to his disciples (that left very formidable livelyhoods to follow Him) how they would be taken care of on this journey. Luke gave up his medical practice, Matthew walked away from a lucrative practice as a tax collector, and the others left various prominent walks-of-life as fishermen and entrepreneurs. He explains that not only will your heavenly Father provide your most basic needs of food and clothing but He gains immense satisfaction from giving you more than mere provisions – God desires to give you the kingdom while you live in this earth.

Jesus says to His new followers: *"Fear not little flock: for it is your Father's good pleasure to give you the Kingdom."* Even more than our earthly fathers, Jesus was saying when my Father gives you His very best it makes Him very happy. A happy God is an incomprehensible thought for many people. Where do they think our drive to be happy comes from? We get it from our Father. This is also why you will never find happiness any where else. Jesus died to bring us back to our only place for true happiness, God our Father, which art in heaven.

Over and over again in the scriptures - the message is clear that we serve a God that is prosperity and pleasure sensitive. In verse 27 of Psalm 35 we see it written about one of His wealthiest servants king David: *"Let the Lord be magnified which hath pleasure in the prosperity of His servant."* There it is again in God's book of facts. The Lord takes pleasure in the prosperity of his people. This is contrary to religious popular opinion. Furthermore, God does not only want to prosper those which are already born with a silver spoon - kings and royalty. He derives an even greater pleasure when through the promise of His word He prospers those which

had only previously known poverty and suffering. This is beauti-
fully outlined in Psalm 149, which is dedicated to the once captive
children of Israel. This was attributed to the now liberated former
prisoners of Egypt, not noble royalty. The admonishment to sing
a new song, rejoice in their king, and praise Him in the dance, is
to God's chosen former slaves.

To exalt these new believers, he writes in verse 4: *"For the Lord
taketh pleasure in his people; He will beautify the meek with salvation."* In essence: This is your new life, now that you are serving
the only true and living God and you no longer worship idols
that could not protect you or free you. So let the high praises of
God always be in your mouth, you can happily rejoice and sing
and dance because the Lord delights in you and He awards your
humility with the beauty of salvation. Their former man-made
golden god's that needed to be milked and fed - and their god's
of marble and stone were only to be worshipped – there was never
any promise of recompense to the worshippers.

Pleasure comes *only* from the seed of the true and living God. It
can only originate from its own kind. Satan, the enemy of our
souls seeks to copycat God's original design and manufactures
imitations to prevent us from experiencing true - divine pleasure.

We certainly cannot argue that there aren't plenty of worldly pleasures, the Bible tells us that too - but they are cheap knock-offs of the designer's original. Everything that God created was good. He noted this after creating the world, its contents, and its vast elements. Then on a related note, after the creation of mankind He remarked that is was very good. Again finding pleasure in what He yielded.

There are demonic forces behind all of the world's super-sized, 33% more, spicy enticements to the Father's design of pleasure.

I am never more irritated than when people claim that this-n-that of today's sinful pleasures are not in the Bible. It may be labeled under innocent titles that soothe our guilty actions. But lust by any other name is still plain old lust. This is valiantly portrayed in Galatians chapter 5. All of the new millennium pornography and lust fits snuggly under the heading of sexual immorality, and sexual immorality is a phony bolony knock-off of God's design for sexual pleasure. Sexual pleasure was only intended to be enjoyed through the union of marriage. Furthermore, Drugs and alcohol are extortions of God's design for the spiritual bliss of salvation. The Devil wants us always looking for a high. If I hear another person say "you can drink as long as you don't get drunk" I don't know what I'll do. Who drinks to not get drunk? Varying states of an altered mind is the reason people drink.

The un-tampered with wine of our lord's first miracle has morphed into the powerfully addicting, elixirs we call today's wine and spirits. Proverbs chapter 20 and verse 1 NLT describes its effect: *"Wine produces mockers, liquor leads to brawls. Whoever is led astray by drink cannot be wise."* Now, more than ever, alcoholics are getting away with the escape route of being supposed "social drinkers". The world now has more so-called social drinkers, social smokers and social sexual deviants than we can cure. Only the God of all creation and everything beautiful knows how to impart the seed of true pleasure to His creation. And consequently, He receives extreme pleasure when we (His likeness) accept the fruit of that seed – salvation through Jesus.

In Genesis Chapter 1, God laid out an unmistakable blueprint of creation for us to follow, whereby we would derive a lifetime of pleasure. And as obvious as it is…I almost missed it. I didn't want you to miss it.

While in the creative mode of Holy operation God spoke the conception of twelve formations into existence. That truly was incredible, but even more astounding was what He used to cause it to materialize. Desiring to follow as closely as possible the blueprint of our Heavenly Father, I thought I was dead on the mark when I activated God's promises with the WORD. It wasn't until I prayed for the true revelation of this did it become instantly recognizable. The Holy Ghost urged me to take a closer look at the scripture. His gentle prompting told me to look specifically at the word God used. I was awe-struck when I saw it. It wasn't so much "the" WORD – rather, it was "a" word. It was the remarkably simple word *LET* that He used to configure the kosmos, or the universe.

From the creation of light, to the creation of every fiber of Adam and Eve's being, God masterfully set into motion the world's twelve point alignment system with the word LET. Twelve times in verses 3 through 27 God commanded the existence of life, order and arrangement - from His incorruptible seed.

1. "Let there be light,
2. Let there be a sky,
3. Let the sky divide the seas from the seas,
4. Let the water beneath the sky be gathered for dry land to appear,

5. Let the earth burst forth with grass and seed bearing plants,

6. Let there be stars in the sky to divide day from night,

7. Let their light shine down upon the earth,

8. Let the waters swarm with fish and other life,

9. Let the skies be filled with birds of every kind,

10. Let the earth bring forth every kind of animal-livestock and small animals,

11. Let us make man in our own image, after our likeness,

12. Let them have dominion over the fish of the sea, and over the fowl of the air, and over the cattle, and over all the earth, and every creeping thing that creeps upon the earth."

Every one of these inspirations was in God, and had to obey his command of LET - and become earthly realities. He was purposeful in His strategy and His objective and concluded His creation at the number twelve. In Biblical history, the number 12 would emerge as the symbol of government, authority, supernatural rule, discipleship, and dominion. This would be the same dominion he gave us in verse 28 of chapter 1. God eliminated any and all excuses that might stifle us – by using a simple uncomplicated yet phenomenally powerful word. He has already done the work, proven the example and supplied the blueprint. All we have to do is use it. He's saying, go ahead, do what I did - you have my permission – take authority, create your existence and take dominion over it! LET His work be perfect!

If your life isn't happening the way you feel it should, it may be because you haven't taken dominion and "Let" it.

God didn't intend the meaning of Let to be let - as in sit back and wait for something to happen. He is putting the onus on us. In its creation form, a simple word like let has powerful affect. It exudes responsibility. Its Hebrew meaning *nathan* (pronounced naw-than') takes on a lot of latitude, to name a few: *to cause, to bring forth, to give, come, to commit, to deliver, to perform to render, to strike, and to thrust.* Any one of these meanings is as powerful as the next – but LET is still simpler. Let, is what He chose to influence our lives. God took charge of the structure of a universe that was already concealed within Him. Likewise the structure of our lives is concealed within us. Another thing that shouldn't be missed is that God's creation brought him much pleasure. Longing for the pleasure only gained through His own image, God sets out to be our example of how to change our void, shapeless, dark world. Throughout the seven day process God routinely encouraged Himself by declaring – His works were good. We are divinely empowered to do the same as our Father.

God all mighty could have done it all without words – He certainly could have done it without *a specific* word. Yet, he chose to arrange the platform of life on earth with the simple word LET. And I almost missed it.

The Haves and The Have Nots

This is another place that I will show you the balance that is so badly needed.

Jesus said in John 10:10 I came that you will have an abundant life. Abundant means more than enough. Webster's Dictionary defines abundant as, affluence, wealth or a relative degree of plentifulness. It means overflowing in provisions, more than enough, and it is clearly the opposite of struggle. In John Chapter 10 verse10 the declaration of abundance is extremely powerful. Our Lord makes it unmistakable that he wants us to live that way. He actually uses Himself (His life) as a barometer for our lives. Jesus boldly declares it as the reason he came to the earth to reverse the inevitable misery, death and final destruction brought by a life under the influence of the thief. He says, *"The thief cometh not, but for to steal, and to kill, and to destroy: "I Am come that they might have life, and that they might have it more abundantly".*

That doesn't sound like I have come that you may have an abundance of struggles. The Body of Christ has to shake loose the "Struggle" mentality which predisposes us to an acceptance of a lifestyle of suffering lack and "Just Getting By". Barely making it does not give glory to God! The time has come for us to grasp the revelation of the haves and denounce the have nots. Jesus died for the privilege for us to have abundance and His dying nailed poverty and lack to the cross…we don't have to live that way. To do so is to live beneath our privilege!

However, it does appear that a lot of Christians have more difficulty with understanding the true manner of suffering that we must bear. Manner of suffering - you mean to say there are categories? Yes - and as a result of the unawareness of such, most of us gladly and readily accept any and all suffering as if it was divinely ordered.

Wearing second hand clothes, driving on bald tires and living at a poverty income level is not the type of suffering that the

Apostle Paul taught we would endure in Second Corinthians 4:8-9. Notice that for every hardship that Apostle Paul describes he gives an exception of what we are *not,* in verse 8 he explains "We are troubled on every side, yet *not* distressed: We are perplexed, but *not* in despair; Persecuted, but *not* forsaken: cast down but *not* destroyed", and even with that much emphasis and specificity we continue to accept any and all manner of suffering (as a way of life) that we were never intended to have.

Paul made it glaringly clear that a lot will happen to us as a result of taking on the life of Christ and confessing Him as Lord and Savior but he also made it just as clear that no matter how bad it gets these five things are concrete promises of what *not* to accept as a way of life: distress, despair, forsaken and destroyed are the "*do nots*" you do not have to accept this as the Christian lifestyle - so why do we? It may be because as Christians, we clearly expect to suffer, so at the first sign of any tribulation we humbly submit.

I guarantee you the persecution and the trouble we will face will be immense, but so will the abundance. We can have it both ways. Since we can't change the "will haves" why not accept everything you "will have" not just the expected hardships: troubled on every side, perplexed, persecuted, and cast down, we will have these without any effort at all but don't leave out the abundance, it too is one of the "will haves" you are entitled to an abundance of prosperity - the promise of abundance should be accepted as part of the unavoidable "will haves" as much as the suffering we will have in our Christians lives.

It's pretty obvious by now that there has to be a balance or rather, there *should* be a balance of wealth as well as spirituality. In order to strike a balance; you must understand, you do not have to have a million dollars to be rich, and people with a million dollars are not necessarily rich – yet God designed it so that we would have it all.

Chapter Four

THE SPIRIT OF LUXURY

The word luxury evokes in our minds a picture of elite living. In this picture, there's a class of people fortunate enough to possess the finer things of life. My experience has shown me that most people definitely do not include themselves in that picture. Luxury makes us think of exclusiveness. To further exclude ourselves from the picture we've all heard the over-zealous preacher assert that God didn't promise us our desires, only our needs. Every Christian should know how seriously God wants to give us our desires: "Delight thyself also in the Lord and He shall give thee the desires of thine heart". Psalms 37:4 suggests a duality of purpose by God, in giving us the things we want, above the things we need.

David clarifies here that God would give us the desires we want as much as establish within us, the things He wants us to want. It looks like one way or another God is making sure that not only your needs are provided, but our desires as well. He shows us that the desires of our heart can be as much ours - as they can be our Fathers'. As we look closer, it becomes clearer that the scripture is conveying that dreaming is imperative. As far as the origin of the dream goes, whether we arrive at it through our own natural sight or that of supernatural is of no real consequence. What God wants us to do is, dare to dream, and dare to believe him for the fulfillment of our dreams. More to the scripture's point, if the dreams are heartfelt and the Lord is our delight, Psalm 37, verse 4 is saying, God will grant us those dreams we desire.

It's a dreadful notion to think that God only wants to give us our basic provisions. It also contradicts the scriptures from Genesis to Revelations. This thinking is responsible for much of the financial lack and poverty plaguing the Body of Christ today. It's a sickness more pervasive than cancer. There is one thing that can affect the root cause of this disease of the mind. That one thing is the Spirit of Luxury.

Regardless of what your religion or personal belief is. There is no one in their right mind that would experience a life of luxury living and trade it for poverty.

Luxury is not about a certain type of décor, be it lavish or be it simple. You can have your simple taste in things and still live the lifestyle we were meant to live on this earth. Luxury also doesn't mean that your trappings or furnishings need to be larger than life or grandiose. The spirit of luxury doesn't make you loose the appreciation for simple things. I love simple things. A life of luxury is often appreciated when less is more. I could certainly settle for a small Rolls Royce parked in front of my small mansion, and a small yacht, docked on my small private island. Yes, less can certainly mean more. Let's face it, life is with a doubt about adjustments – but it's much better to adjust up than to adjust down.

If we won't believe that God wants to give us luxury and abundance, we certainly couldn't believe that He wants us to have it routinely. Just sprinkle a little luxury down on us every now and then and we'll be happy. That makes more sense to us, because we really don't believe we're entitled to a lifetime of luxury anyway – that would be too excessive. Thank God that's not what the scripture says. In Jeremiah chapter 31, verse 5 KJV - God says to His people through the prophet Jeremiah *"You shall yet plant vines upon the mountains of Samaria: the planters shall plant, and shall eat them as common things"*. God did not intend for luxury to be rare. A lifestyle of luxury living should be as common to us as a change of clothes. Furthermore, luxury is not something dispersed to us randomly, with no real aim or plan for whom God will bless. God has a real plan and intention to repay His people for their dedication to His Kingdom. Proverbs 11:31 speaks to this fact: *"Behold, the righteous shall be recompensed in the earth: much greater than the wicked.*

Gift giving and receiving should not only be reserved for special occasions. It should become a common thing. Everyday fine dining - with all the trimmings is not just for Thanksgiving. Waiting to buy a new car, only when the old clunker gives out is not only mind-boggling - it's ridiculous. Spouses hiding their new purchases from their curious better-halves just to keep the peace – this should be a thing of the past. The most popular defense for living this way is "I don't have expensive taste, and most of these things are overpriced anyway." Don't worry; your high-end faith will change your low-end taste, faith is priceless.

High prices are just another opportunity for you to extend your faith. Faith is not just for salvation and healing. Now that you're saved and your body is healthy, what are you going to use your faith for? We just saw in Psalm 37:4 that God divinely gives you desires to exalt your faith to higher levels. If you don't want a luxury car, or a luxury home, that's still no excuse. God holds us all responsible for the advancement of His kingdom. He holds us responsible for feeding the poor, caring for the widows as well as spreading the Gospel. There is no getting around it. You still have the responsibility of demonstrating faith in God. What will your faith produce?

The other high ranking excuse for this kind of thrifty living is: "the economy is bad". Despite the politicians spin, there is nothing wrong with the economy. This earth has a never-ending supply of resources to sustain us, as well as bring us wealth. The true reason for this sub-standard thinking is because the faith that produces a lifestyle of luxury is uncommon. It's much easier to live ordinary than to live extraordinary. When you learn the superior advantage of the word of God, ordinary will never satisfy you. The greatest appreciation of receiving the word of God is shown in your operation of it. To operate in this kind of conviction is a superior level of faith.

Time For Wine

In the Gospel of John 2:1-11 KJV Jesus goes to a wedding feast. There He was, as dashingly handsome as the Proverbs 22:19 man he is. His beauty truly His kindness. Mingling among the guest and socializing, in as much human being as spirit being –enjoying Himself. Always the example for us to follow - Jesus was not too holy to be entertained, nor was He too pious to do a two step. His Holiness was not so religious that He couldn't enjoy His Mission-charged life. Sure He had a purpose, and He was on a mission, but He gave His Father pleasure while He was about His Father's business. Jesus knew how to hang – He knew how to chill. It may come as quite a surprise to some, but Jesus had a sense of humor, he even cracked jokes – and like most shameless comics, He probably laughed at His own jokes too.

There is a miserable life to be had when we, the anointed follow our own lead, instead of His.

In the midst of the celebration Mary, Jesus' mother told Him that they had run out of wine. Jesus, being respectful, but unbothered by the cause comes back with, "what does that have to do with you and me?" "My time has not yet come." Without any hesitation, as if she hadn't heard him – Mary instructs the servants to do whatever He tells them. This was the first miracle of Jesus that was recorded in the New Testament. Mary asked and Jesus gave. She had faith that He would provide for her and He did.

Many ask God for things but regardless of what their mouths are saying their hearts are dancing to different tune. Asking God for things but having no real faith that He will come through, is another reason for unanswered prayers.

Mary, *"mother of Jesus!"* should be more than just a pre cursor to swearing. We need to display her faith attitude. Hers was the faith that ignored the appearance of adversity, and focused only on he fulfillment of the need. Her faith insisted that Her Holy son's first miracle commence.

Our savior's first miracle was not a necessity. It was an indulgence. This was clearly a miracle of increase and luxury. Wine being symbolic of luxury, joy and judgment. Jesus improved the wine as well as increased it. He didn't give them just a little wine. He gave them more than enough. He told them to fill the water pots to the brim and they obliged. They believed that Jesus could increase the wine. He, like His Father, always gave more than He was asked. Jesus would have given them Nappa Valley if there was more time.

He filled their pots to the brim, not half way or three-quarters of the way, but a supernatural overflow.

Why not ask God for something "big"? For once in your life, ask God for what you really want. If you're tired of your present mode of transportation why would you ask God for just a car when it's His pleasure to give you the car of your hearts desire. You cannot ask God for too much.

The kingdom of God does not function like WAL-MART or your local grocer that needs to constantly restock their shelves. Heaven's supply is inexhaustible. Take a leap of faith and be specific. God loves the details. But be assured that those details will launch you into a "mother of Jesus" realm of faith. So go for it! He can give you more than you can ever imagine or hope for. Every time you put your faith on the line to get the desires you really want, it gives God pleasure. He rejoices, because they were His desires in the first place.

Jesus could have opened the blind eyes, healed the sick or raised the dead but He chose not to do any of those things first. God had this miracle designed for the religious traditionalists. He knew the minds of the holier-than-thou pious nations of that day, and this day. The ones that say all they need is Jesus, their true desires hidden behind their fear of failure. They don't realize their only failure is in being faithless. This miracle of luxury and increase was tailor made for them. Veronica's miracle, opening blind eyes, and reviving Lazarus would have to wait. A much less sacred, yet just as affecting miracle would take precedence.

It would take a miracle of luxury to crush the religious critic's rumors about Jesus. His opponents knew He was wealth personified, though they'd never admit it. Drawing wine from water would prove it. Jesus knew that the self-righteous would claim that being spiritual meant being without. A miracle of luxury would contradict their irreverence. This miracle was clearly one of "excess". If He hadn't performed this miracle first, the church would have confused the purpose of wealth - and thought it was something not intended for Christians. God forbid.

Jesus was sending a strong statement at this wedding. This miracle would give Him an infinitely greater start than any other could. Opening deaf ears and healing leprosy wouldn't have the same affect on our future had He performed them first. Verse 11 not only declares this a miracle of priority, but the scripture points to this as the miracle that first displayed the savior's glory. This is Phenomenal! Our Lord had just left the wilderness after forty days and nights and won a battle over the devil. And yet, His Father did not reveal His son's Glory, or even call it a miracle. But He did with luxury. By choosing wine before healing, our Father boldly leveled the natural with the spiritual.

The striking and infinite message He sent to our human culture is that luxury awaits your wilderness. No matter how wild your wilderness gets…luxury awaits.

This miracle also flies in the face of one of the greatest misconceptions out today. We've all said it ourselves – God is not materialistic. To be fair He's not, at least not in the commercial sense. Yet, we know that heaven has material blessings galore. Every precious gem, metal and material imaginable is the very setting of heaven.

Let's face it; your faith will produce tangible things - as well as intangible. The faithful should no more feel guilty for their new car and clothes than the new Christian for their salvation.

Jesus disposes more earthly misconceptions in the performance of this miracle. The other is about how single-minded God is. The entire Bible proves that to be a false perception. He made a mate for Adam so that he and Eve would be a couple. He ordered Noah to put passengers on the ark in doubles. He made goodness and mercy our convoy for this life; and He justified heaven and earth with Father and Son. He wanted to stabilize our understanding of the natural and the spiritual. He's not single-minded, He's balanced-minded. And this miracle screams at us to understand that God always provides a perfect balance for us to live by. Luxury is spiritual, and luxury, like healing, has deep intrinsic value.

This miracle also symbolized a breaking of tradition; because it was part of Jewish tradition to wash your hands before and after a meal. Jesus used the water that they were to wash their hands with to make the wine. Given that water is the symbol for the spirit - by using the water for a purpose other than it was intended, Jesus fearlessly reassigned the way we would view the Holy Spirit. When they poured that beautiful wine it symbolized that the Holy Spirit could not be contained within the walls of temples, or on precious untouchable tablets. It most definitely is not to be contained in the dormant minds of the religious. As chief corner stone and foundation, He was establishing the foundation for Christianity, to be unrestrained and uncontained. It had to be poured, and poured upon all flesh. And all flesh had to be filled, filled with His spirit.

As Jesus began to draw out that beautiful, pure, fresh, wine it was apparent that it was the best they ever had. When the Master of Ceremony tasted the wine he was astounded. It was so good. The Living Bible says he remarked "Oh what wonderful stuff." He said the best wine was saved for last. It was wonderful stuff.

Jesus' first miracle of wonderful stuff draws a striking parallel to Moses' first miracle. Moses the lawgiver turns water into blood (Exodus 7:14-14). The blood was a symbol of judgment. Jesus the grace giver turns water into wine. The wine was a symbol of judgment, Joy and luxury. Jesus' miracle dispenses joy and luxury instead of just judgment. A feat only pulled off by grace. Moses instituted the law first, which was good. Jesus ushered in grace which is infinitely better. Moses' law was the old covenant, it came first – Jesus is the new covenant (and the new wine) He would be the first, and the last.

It was also customary to serve the best wine first and save the rest for last, we see here that the last was better than the first.

God, the Alpha and Omega, wants to increase you, and will make a way to get prosperity to you – according to your faith.

A Thousand Pictures…worth all the words

Superior faith is developed when you exercise your faith with action. From whatever faith level you are at; according to your faith - the lifestyle God desires for you is yours for the taking.

Here is what Paul taught the church at Ephesus: "Now glory be unto God that is able to do exceedingly abundantly above all that we ask or think, according to the power that is at work in us, Ephesians 3:20 KJV. The power he's talking about is faith. God is able to, and will go beyond what you ask based on the strength of your faith. According to your faith God will do extraordinarily more than you can ask or even think. Your faith is the benchmark that God uses to go above and beyond for you.

It's a good idea to have a picture of the strength of your faith. Understanding different faith levels is nothing new. The Bible is a photo gallery of thousands of pictures of faith. A picture of where your faith is can help you finally picture *yourself* living in the "spirit of luxury". I've already shown you one of those pictures using a page from Jesus' own personal album. His mother Mary produced a particular level of faith almost unseen today. On at least two occasions she ignored adverse information brought to her and proceeded on to do according to that which was planned for destiny. In one of those incidents, after being told by her son the Messiah that he was not particularly concerned with displaying His Glory at a wedding function, she pursues her own intentions. She exercised the faith that would do above that which she asked. Thanks to Mary, wine has never been sweeter since that day.

More than that, she is recognized as a spiritual icon today, because of her faith in God she would immaculately conceive our savior. The truth that she as a virgin conceived Jesus is not the only miracle. What was also miraculous was that *she* was the one chosen. The first chapter of Luke verse 30 says that Mary found favor with God.

Mary possessed the faith characteristics that proved her to be the only eligible agent for Christ's conception and birth. The characteristic that God favored in Mary is more than virginity (although greatly revered, during that time) it was the rarely demonstrated holiness that God so favored in her. Mary truly lived holy, and what was almost impossible at that time - she was not self-righteous about it. Every childbearing woman of that time hoped to be the famed woman of prophecy. Every virgin in and around Israel hoped to be the one chosen to birth the Messiah. I'm sure Mary was no different; she wasn't so out of touch that she wouldn't have wanted what all other women wanted. But she wasn't arrogant. The scripture says (Luke 1:29) when Gabriel (the angel) told her that she was highly favored by God and blessed among women – she was confused and disturbed. That's because she was not expecting this exhortation.

Unlike many of us, Mary wasn't flaunting her holy status – publicizing every time she prayed. The scripture doesn't even say that she bragged about her virginity. She didn't toot her own horn, conceited that she had a closeness with God that no one else had. Mary was humble, she was holy, she was innocent, she loved God, and she was chosen. All of the above are characteristics of faith. Sounds simple – yet it is more often said than done.

While living holy is a leading characteristic of true faith, in the same way, sin sucks the faith right out of your soul. The servant of God that lives in a constant state of sin rarely believes God for anything. That's why the Apostle Paul stressed it so emphatically; in his first letter to Apostle Peter. In Chapter 2 and verse 11: he writes that *"it wars against the soul."* A holy surrendered life unto God is not to be taken for granted. Mary lived a completely surrendered life, and it is no wonder why she had a part in the first miracle as well as the most essential part in He that would be the first and the last.

No Faith?

There are more pictures in the gallery of people that displayed varying strengths in faith. It seems inconsistent to ponder no faith being included in this line up, it even seems impossible. However, the Bible shows us it is possible to have "no" faith. What picture gallery would be complete without snapshots of the bad things as well as the good? Deuteronomy chapter 32 verse 20 spells out to us just how this is possible.

"And he said, I will hide my face from them, I will see what their end shall be: for they are a very froward generation, in whom is no faith." The God of all that is good, that freed a captive people and made provisions for their lives and their generations was now angry at their ungrateful disrespect. The preceding verse gives us the picture of what brought it on. Verse 15 is the most frightening depiction for us to learn from, it says: "They forsook God which made them". "They forsook the God of their salvation; they made a mockery of their salvation". Now that they were eating the fat of lambs, fresh pancakes and drinking the juice of the choice grapes; they deserted the true and living God and abandoned their salvation for new gods that had just arrived.

This is evidence of why faith cannot reign where sin abounds? God detested their deeds and labeled them as having *no faith*. When you forsake righteousness you forsake your faith. There is no way to clean this up and call it anything else but what God Himself called it – no faith. No faith means more than a failure to believe, it underscores the truth that you are without a covering, literally without God. Even when Israel thought they could erect gods to their own satisfaction, it was still no contest for the power of the rock of salvation. God is the only God – and anything else is as having no God – or no faith. Verse 17 says they sacrificed unto devils.

The world's unwillingness to recognize God may not be as obvious as theirs; but it is just as much a sacrifice unto devils as theirs. Israel's worst offence was not just the fact that they forsook God and turned from Him, but they were a nation that forgot the God that created them, and delivered them, now there would be an even worse fate. God turned from *them*! God hides His face from the deplorable state of those that renounce Him.

This sounds harsh doesn't it? Yet, what our Holy God says next is harsher. At the top of verse 20 we heed a very strong warning from a jealous God: *"I will hide my face from them, and see to their end."* That is, I will see to their doom, I will cause their destruction.

No point in trying to comfort the Godless into believing that God understands…because He doesn't. He's jealous. And He has a right to be, He made us, and He has a zero tolerance when He is provoked.

As a senior pastor, such as pastor Moses was, I've learned that the faithless is certainly not the excuseless. Every week I'm confronted with a litany of reasons as the excuses people use for their sacrifice to devils. Every thing from, my job is too demanding of my time, to, I had to do the laundry or I had to wash my car, are the excuses people use that have abandoned the God of their salvation.

Why should a pastor expect people to come to church on Sunday and spend more than an hour worshipping? Why don't they just leave people alone? Isn't the church in our hearts anyway? God understands that we need proper rest for the week ahead. Moses had as many of these excuses and complaints and more.

The unpleasant yet unyielding answer to why is permanently stamped into God's book of facts. Verse 46 and 47 of this chapter tells us precisely why we cannot leave people alone. Pastor Moses bounces back from the complaints of his faithless and thankless followers. While under the guiding of the Holy God he addresses the children of Israel before he goes to die: ***"Set your hearts unto all the words which I testify among you this day, which ye shall command your children to observe to do, all the words of this law. For it is not in vain for you; because it is your life; and through this thing ye shall prolong your days in the land, when you go over Jordan to possess it."***

The reasons why good balanced preachers can't let up is clear.

The number 1 reason why is in v46: ***"set your hearts unto all the words that I have given you today."*** As Pastor Moses did, God requires of us to set/condition your hearts. We must prepare your hearts to do everything that God commanded, and preaching the Gospel is the only way to do that. Also like Moses, we are required to command you to pass it on. The Gospel truth is not left up to only those who hear it and preach it now – but those that will hear it later. It was not over when Moses was dead, it's generational, and it's eternal, and regardless of how the world has been de-sensitized to Godlessness we must continue to proclaim the truth until the end.

The number 2 reason why we can't let up is in v47: ***"For it is not a vain thing for you;"*** Other things may seem more important or more logical in your own understanding, but God didn't want Moses to leave their journey up to their own understanding. The world left up to their own wisdom and understanding did not come to know God says Apostle Paul in 1 Corinthians 1:21. Man at his best, despite all of his religious and intellectual accomplishments would not ever come close to the knowledge of God. That's why we preach the Gospel. And that's why God says it is not in vain. He wanted them to know that their obedience and servitude to God is not in vain. For sure we don't always immediately see the affects of sharing the Gospel, but the least thing done for the kingdom of God is the greatest thing we can do for mankind – and is never in vain or a waste of time.

The number 3 reason why we can't let up is also in v47: *"because it is your life and through this thing ye shall prolong your days in the land, when you go over Jordan to possess it"*. Your life, your very existence depends on your obedience to God's laws: and by obeying them you will enjoy a long and prosperous life in the land that God promised you – and God will lengthen the days of your life because of your obedience. Also by doing so, you will own it, possess it, and have dominion over it.

These are the unfailing reasons why I/we cannot let up. It is ultimately to keep you from the disaster of having no faith.

The New Testament, the Gospel of Mark, Chapter 4 verse 40 pictures Jesus giving the disciples a spiritual eye opener for being faithless. And He said unto them, "Why are ye so fearful?" How is it that ye have no faith?" He actually says: "Why are ye so fearful? How is it that ye have no faith"? Jesus asked this question because He knew His disciples, and He knew they did not possess characteristics of having no faith – so what was causing this false appearance? Fear!

The Messiah not only asked them how they became so faithless, He also questioned how they could be so afraid. Their gripping fear of surrounding circumstances rendered them temporarily faithless. They allowed their five senses to give them the same resemblance of someone which had denounced the living God, no better than idol worshippers, or those that sacrifice to devils.

The paralyzing affects of fear puts your trust in God at a stand still. Be assured that true faith never fails. It would be a lie if I said I've never been afraid. All of us, especially my self have been absorbed by the fear of one thing or another.

That being said, fear cannot withstand faith in God. Fortunately, God does not wash His hands of us because we become fearful and faithless. Jesus rebuked the cause of their fear (the wind and the sea) rather than rebuking them for their fear. He gave them the prescription for their future fears. The word of God! Instead of joining the faithless as many of us do, He took a stance alone and used faith-fortified intense words. His words out of our mouths, is the formula for fear to bow its knees to faith. Use as directed.

Just A Little Faith

Do you believe that God will provide your most basic necessities in life? Everyone answers that question with an overwhelming - absolutely yes. No one wants to be classified as having only a little faith. My scientific data (pastoring) shows this to be the case. Contrary to most people's claim to be of great faith – the overwhelming evidence proves, we're not. Food, shelter, clothes and work, for the sustenance of life is what most serious believers distrust God for. If my goal is truly to get you to the place of believing God for the uncommon – spiritual as well as natural wealth. I must make you aware of the common. I am duty bound to alert you of the risk of having only a little faith. I'll first make my case clear by informing you that it's not just my claim when I amusingly say that my scientific data proves most to be of a little faith. The Bible's scientific data reveals that when challenged by the opposition of just getting our basic needs met – our faith falters.

Let's re-visit Jesus as He wrestles with the irrational fears of His Jewish converts. In chapter 6 of the Gospel of Matthew, He would address an assortment of basic needs. After He reshapes their thinking with His moving B-attitudes - He expounds His deep Sermon on the Mount, on being a hypocrite, on prayer and fasting, on loving your enemies, on earthly treasures and daily living. Not too wide an array for the master teacher. He first garners their support and favor by addressing the expected, in His famous sermon; finishing up with a call for them to be perfect. He then hits them with the unexpected in verse 30. The master, wiser than King Solomon as promised - waits until their motivation is at an all-time high to deliver the bombshell of change. *"You have so little faith!"* He proposes, as He pronounces their disbelief in their Father's ability to make everyday provisions. As He teaches them,

He reaches them, and they just barely and mercifully escape the disgraceful ranking of being of *no faith*.

Being of little faith is the failure to believe God for your basic necessities. To fall into this category is to not trust Him for the air that you breathe. Jesus wanted to shake them into understanding - if you can't trust God for the simplest of needs, how will you ever believe that He will prepare a place for you in His Father's kingdom – which is harder to believe? Or, if you can't believe Him for food and clothing, how will you believe that faith in Him could free you from the temptations of the flesh? Which of these is easier to believe?

A spiritual shaking is often the awakening we need to reveal our faith status. To ensure that they got it, He offered them a picture of the Father's love comparing His care for them against His care for flowers. But not just any flowers, lilies, the very flower depicted in the Old Covenant and in the New, this was our savior's best hope for explaining God's care. In the book of Hosea chapter 14, verse 5 God simulates the deliverance of Israel. His depiction of their rescue is described as the refreshing dew from heaven. The NLT says of the once captive people: *"It will blossom like the lily."* The way the lily blossoms is the way He wants His people to thrive. Only a master of men and matter would think to use such a flower. One that lives among the wheat, a symbol of the word of God adorned with strikingly beautiful colors having a piously regal stance. Pink, purple, violet, and indigo, pick a color, they're all in heaven. So is the lily, if I know anything about our Father's love for beauty. Some species of the lily grow everywhere, even wild among standing corn, another symbol of God's truth, no coincidence there. Of all the beautiful flowers no other was worthy of this comparison of love. The lily fit all the pre-requisites to be chosen to illustrate God's care for His children.

Strong resilient and wild, yet beautiful and vulnerable, in desperate need of a savior – just like us. Just as God knows everything, everything knows God. The lily must know that just one of them is more exceptional in appearance than all of Solomon's great works – and that's why they exist. The lily knows that its purpose for being is to serve as a reminder to us of the weight of our Father's care for us; they would have to be beautiful to do that.

Jesus was saying in Matthew 6:28-29 the next time you doubt the Father's care for your needs think about my due diligence in choosing the lilies, and they don't offer nearly as much as why I chose you. Yet I made sure that their beauty is more exceptional than all the works of Solomon. We give the Father more than the mere distinctness of our beauty. We are His image, His likeness. He left that unique distinction only to be fulfilled by man kind. In exchange for such a high ranking, He expects us to hold the superior position of having more than just - a little faith.

If He cares so much for lilies which offer no more than beauty at-a-glance, then your faith is minuscule if you don't think he cares more for you.

What Great Faith!

The Gospel of Matthew 15:28 unveils a faithful woman of Canaan that demonstrates to us what great faith is. Great faith people don't try Jesus...they trust Jesus. For these people there is no other alternative, no plan "B", it's Jesus and Him only. Those that exercise this level of faith, often don't have many resources. The once financially independent often find themselves lacking the independence in which they had worked so hard for. People that operate in "great faith" are not necessasarily considered to be great people – and are almost always alone in their faith endeavors.

This faith supercedes your personal condition, your present surroundings, and any opposition to your intentions.

This Canaan woman had already taken that rare introspective look at her self and accepted who and what she was. She was a Gentile, understood to be impure, unclean, a dog. She also knew that Jews had the rare and distinct honor to be classed as God's depository of His truth. This distinction would only be for a time if she had anything to do with it. She would daringly place herself in the bond of covenant of Abraham by her willingness to beseech Jesus.

Now here is a woman who knew who she was; she knew what her mission was. She also knew Jesus wasn't being politically incorrect when He referred to her as a dog. That mattered nothing at all to her. Jesus wasn't degrading her, He wasn't a woman basher nor was He being politically incorrect. They lived in a different time than the over indulgent, "me" generation of a world we live in now. It was not considered to be disrespectful to refer to someone by their class, national origin, or race. A Centurion, a ruler, Matthew the Publican, Simon the Canaanite, the Canaan woman, a Jew, a Gentile – just a few titles of recognition frequently used. A Canaanite was commonly referred to as a dog, it was an accepted way of identifying the unelected, the un-chosen. Jesus was simply accurately acknowledging and even recognizing her class in life. But she would change that.

Her daughter's possession by devils outweighed what He thought of her anyway. Who cares if you're known for your many petitions for deliverance? It shouldn't matter that you continue to pray for the same miracle until you see it manifested. Isaiah's prayer for Jerusalem in chapter 62:6-7 pleaded: *"I have set watchmen on thy walls, O Jerusalem, which shall never hold their peace day nor night: ye that make mention of the Lord, keep not silence. And give him no rest, till he establish, and till he make Jerusalem a praise in the earth."* Until your problem becomes a praise, don't stop praying.

She pleaded mercifully for His help. This should do it she thought *"thou son of David"* she begged. Verse 23 says *"But He answered her not"*, she couldn't even get His attention by recognizing His place in the royal tree of David. Even that did not get her what she wanted.

I see this all the time, people wasting precious time recognizing all the beauty of His deity instead of plainly asking for what they need. "Oh honorable, eternal, gracious glorious, loving, merciful, heavenly father", is an unnecessary prelude for talking to your father. If sincere, it may get God's attention, but many undergo this excessiveness because it gets the attention of their earthly audience. Try calling on him using the description that was dearly paid for…Father, in the name of Jesus.

Annoyed by her persistence, the disciples try to silence her attempts. Verse 23 exposes the condition of their hearts in the presence of her dire need. The master was now very popular, a celebrity and they had become conceited, shadowing the master – backseat driving on all His victories. *"Master she's bothering us with all that begging"* they shouted. *"Send her away!"* Come on, who were they kidding - she wasn't after them, for what she needed – they could only be a poor substitute not even a close second. Her daughter needed a major miracle, and she needed more than second fiddle. So she worshipped! Right then and there ignoring his disciples and ignoring her status, only reverencing His. She worships. This would get a rise out of the Master, now Jesus tells her the truth – and she calls him the TRUTH. He reminds her that the time to offer the power of His ministry to dogs hasn't come yet. She cleverly answers Him *"TRUTH Lord, but even dogs (Gentiles) can partake of the crumbs from the master's table"*.

Her worship unleashed the faith she needed for her miracle. Her faith was now exposed. Now Jesus would see what was invisible to the natural eye. She didn't just tell the truth, she told Him *He* was the truth. Only great faith could have recognized this. His own disciples thought it was them she cried after. Once His distinction was revealed, Jesus was committed to her daughter's deliverance. Jesus replied, *"O woman great is thy faith: be it unto you even as you wish"*. Her daughter was immediately made whole. When you are able to go beyond insurmountable odds, beyond yourself and only see Jesus as the means to your end – that is great faith.

So Great Faith!

If we've learned anything up to this point, we've learned that these snapshots reveal that we don't know as much as we thought we did about faith. There is still much more to learn. Remember how we were taught in grade school to apply increasing values? We were taught that *great* was good but *greater* was better, and better still was *greatest*. Levels of faith are applied in the same way. So far we've looked at *no faith, little faith and great faith*. What's more important is that I've shown you this from the word of God and not my opinion. Let's look at how the Word portrays the phenomenal *so great faith*.

This greatest level of faith is when you rely on the word *only* - from wherever you are for deliverance in any situation.

Matthew 8:5 reveals the uncommon "so great faith". Although this level of faith is discovered during our Lord's early ministry, it is not a stretch to say that Jesus never saw any greater faith before or after this captain of rank in the Roman army. His request for our Lord to heal his paralyzed servant was granted without reservation by Jesus. This brings to question why? Why did Jesus act so immediately when beseeched by this Centurion? The Gospel that parallels this is Luke chapter 7 verses 4 and 5, which vividly portrays the answer to that question.

Verse 4 tells us; ***"And when they came to Jesus, they besought him instantly, saying, That he was worthy for whom he should do this:"*** There's the answer, he was found worthy. What humility the centurion shows – he didn't think himself worthy to entreat Jesus - but the highest of Jewish elders did, and would make haste to defend his honor. The only thing that could command this kind of reaction and immediate attention is the two things cited next in verse 5.

"For he loveth our nation, and he hath built us a synagogue." Look at what love does! Love gives, without parameters, without boundaries and without measure he gave above his natural affinity. A Commander of the fierce Roman army (known to be detractors of early Christianity) sends the high ranking elders of the Jews to Jesus to beg of Him to heal his dying servant. And they make hast to do it, simply because he loved Israel and he demonstrated his love with his time and money. This Centurion loved the Jews, God's chosen people. Above his training and any natural affinity with his own people that hated the Jews, he openly showed an outpouring of affection for Israel.

There is no point trying to get around what it takes to have the greatest of faiths – it takes love -unconditional, unselfish First Corinthians chapter 13 love. This love moved Jesus! Love moves the favor of God in the miraculous for you.

It seems allowable to infer that not love alone but love for the people of God as seen in Matthew 8:7 is what caused such an instant response from our Lord. Jesus knew that you can't love God if you don't love his people.

Verse 5 of Luke chapter 7also cites the one and only other thing that it took for the Lord to name this as the greatest of faith levels...*"and he hath built us a synagogue."* The very synagogue in which Jesus would regularly teach was built by this man of so great faith. What on earth does that have to do with faith you ask? It has everything to do with it.

He wasn't trained in our way of faith – to believe in an invisible God. His faith relied on many gods, for many things, gods tendered by hand that he could see and feel. But it was those gods that would fail him when his dear servant was near death. By building a place of prayer and worship this captain of men put his faith in the God of the people he had come to love.

How much time does it take to build a synagogue anyway? It certainly took more time in that day than it does now. I submit that more than bricks and mortar were being laid during the construction phase. Those faithful Jewish converts were laying the foundation of faith in the centurion's soldier's heart. And by the time the synagogue was finished, so was his allegiance to those Roman gods. Now his faith in the son of God would be manifested.

And how much money does it take to build a synagogue? Whatever the monetary costs no price was too great for his so great faith. Don't take working for the Kingdom of God lightly. Kingdom work has serious long lasting reward. The work that was begun in this courageous centurion still continues today according to

Philippians 1:6 *"Being confident of this very thing, that he which hath begun a good work in you will perform it until the day of Jesus Christ".* Jesus viewed his request as priority one – because he loved His people and he gave with the intention of advancing the kingdom. So at the officer's request, Jesus replied in an instant *"I will come and heal him."*

The centurion's belief was that he was not worthy of Jesus' personal attention in that way. He knew what it meant to have authority and to be under authority, and that respect of Jesus' importance forced his faith into *'speak the word only gear'.* This wasn't hard or unusual for him – it was the word *only* that had gotten him to this rarely seen position of faith he was now in. Remember verse 5 says - he loved the people of God – and he built a synagogue, this was birth from the initiative of the word *only.* He already knew the power and authority of the rich word of God from the people he loved, the Christian Jews. Written or spoken nothing was more powerful than the word of God. Although up to this point he had never heard the word spoken from the master speaker.

Verse 8 of the NLT says he said this: "Lord I am mot worthy to have you come to my home, *just say the word from where you are,* and my servant will be healed!" The faith to believe God for the miraculous from where *you* are – whatever the condition, whatever the prognosis, wherever that impossible circumstance may be - is where the faith that moves mountains is.

The scripture says that when Jesus heard this he marveled. He marveled at his respect for the importance of Jesus' word, as well as how much value he placed on Jesus' authority – and Jesus' ministry. The word *only* would be all he needed, to believe that the deadly affects of his friend's palsy had ended.

Who of us would decline an opportunity for the Lord of Lords to come to our home to do His mission work? Not only do we expect our local Pastors to come to our house, but to the house of our friends and family, and our neighbors and their family, and so on. And if that's not enough there is a progressing belief that the church should be building *our* houses, and sending our children to college and more. We place enormous unwarranted responsibility on the church, when our faith pales in comparison to that of the faith of this centurion officer. Ask yourself, have you displayed the *so great* faith - do you love not only all people (which everybody says until they experience all people) but God's chosen people as well? And what have you done lately to build the church?

The 10th verse says that it was then, (after Jesus knew who he was) that Jesus turned to the crowd and said: *"Verily I say unto you, I have not found so great faith, no not in Israel"*. No greater faith anywhere, not even in Israel? Jesus made a powerful indictment on those once thought to be of the greatest faith. Let's see, His own mother was in Israel, and we know she had a strong faith attitude. Don't forget the disciples were in Israel too, and not even they measured up to the greatest faith ever seen by our savior. But a rich, non-Christian, Roman officer's did. His faith was greater than great, and greater than the greatest, it was SO GREAT!

Chapter Five

LIVING THE RICH AND HOLY LIFESTYLE

With the spirit of luxury comes responsibility. The responsibility of having wealth on this earth and living righteously is a very delicate balance to weigh. As much as people try to rationalize their denial of our need for wealth; the truth still remains. We will not need money in heaven – truth is, we won't have financial responsibilities in heaven. Mortgages, car loans, and even credit, we will have no use for in heaven. Gone will be the days of saving to pay college tuition, there won't be any need for saving. The need for college won't even exist, by then we will know all things as Jesus does. Yes, we will all be blessed in heaven. But It's here on earth where we need to prosper and I've shown you that God wants His children to live in prosperity.

The answer to exactly how we go about acquiring prosperity is a study in the man that started it all. A friend of God and a man that unconditionally trusted the promises of God - originally known as Abram. Abraham was the first of the patriarchs of Israel. Along with Abraham's great wealth he exercised great faith in God. God found favor in Abraham and promised him that He would bless him. Throughout the Bible the name Abraham has become synonymous with great faith in God.

Abraham was very rich in cattle and silver and gold. In those days your cattle measured your wealth, which would have made Abraham a cattle mogul. He wasn't just rich, but as I noted in a previous chapter he was extremely rich. Not only was Abraham rich but his family was also rich. The book of Genesis says that when Abraham left the land of Ur with his wife that he had his nephew Lot with him. He had so many cattle, that he and Lot were not able to graze on the same land. Their wealth was so immense that the land was not able to support them. Still his humility was unsurpassed by any, and not affected at all by his wealth. Genesis 14:20 reveals that out of sheer love and humility to the king of Salem, Melchezedeck; he paid a tenth of all he had to the high priest. That's right of all he had! Of all of his gold, of all of his silver and unlike many of today's wealthy, a tenth of all of his greatest wealth, his cattle.

This was an amazing feat not because his wealth was so immense, but because he was not duty-bound by God to pay tithes. He was the real honest Abe. He purposely invented the responsibility of tithing for himself and was not required to do so. This calls to question, how much kingdom responsibility above our reasonable service – are we willing to invent for our selves? Whatever the amount, we'll make friends in heaven.

The Lord spoke to him in Haran, after leaving Ur of the Chaldeans (present day Iraq) and told him to leave his country and all his relatives and vacate the comfort of his father's house. Without any hesitation Abraham obeyed. He didn't allow the hindrances of transportation, communication or the absence of a hint from God about where he would end up to a hamper his voyage. Even today a distance of a few hundred miles from Haran to Canaan (present day Israel) his final destination - would require some geographical knowledge, of which Abraham had none. God's supernatural plan was to uproot Abraham and transplant a nation within a nation. Abraham possessed phenomenal faith in God. His is the kind of faith almost never seen today, reminiscent only of Christ

Himself. Genesis chapter 15 verse 6 says Abraham's faith in God was counted as righteousness. Abraham was obedient to a fault, and when God told him to give up his son he did it. After it took him 100 years to get Isaac God said give him back to me.

Abraham's faith was solid. He didn't bargain with God or try to rationalize and dissect what God really meant by sacrifice like some of us. "Does He really mean sacrifice as in slay him or does He mean sacrifice as in do not put Isaac before God?" Abraham knew his Heavenly Father well enough to know what He meant. He didn't rationalize away the real meaning. The only sacrifice that was worthy enough, would unveil the faith that was in Abraham; and that was what God was asking for and nothing less.

Thank God Abraham was not like us desperately searching for a logical conclusion to why God would require a sacrifice of the very thing we love the most. The simple but hard to accept truth is - - God is not logical. It's not logical to love your enemies, it's not logical to give before you get, or believe what you cannot see. No, it's not logical - and His patriarch of faith knew that. Abraham knew exactly what God meant give Isaac back to me. Not some "hypothetically speaking" figurative sacrifice of his love or devotion to Isaac – but Isaac's life. God was constraining him to literally offer his son's life to him. This was supernaturally sensitive!

Now Abraham would have to balance his love for his most precious gift (his son Isaac) with his love of his most precious God. He was one hand-stroke away from Isaac's throat – the lad was sure to meet his demise when the Lord saw that He feared him - more than he feared losing his only son. So the Lord provided a substitute – for Isaac and for the lamb – He would be sacrificed later. For now, a ram would have to do.

When God requires a sacrifice of us it can only yield a blessing of supernatural proportions. Only when Abraham willingly sought to take Isaac's life for a sacrifice did God reaffirm the Abrahamic covenant. He initiated His covenant with him in Genesis chapter 12 verses 1-4. In chapter 22 God wasn't just restating the covenant he was instating the covenant. It took the action of the sacrifice to inaugurate the promise. And as with any inauguration of promise, a symbolic memorial bearing the name of the occasion is given. Abraham declared the name of that place Jehovah–Jireh: *The Lord will provide or see.* Just another way Abraham showed that he loved His God.

Our responsibility is our willingness to be obedient concerning the sacrifice. It took the willingness of a father to surrender his one beloved son for him to become the father of all sons. Any great mark made in biblical history began with a sacrifice. But a sacrifice must always be birth out of love, and love always gives. The way to gain is to give. Abraham gave. He gave tithes to Melchezedek when he was not required to. He gave Isaac to be sacrificed. Out of these amazing feats of expressive giving Abraham became the recipient of a global covenant that we are partakers of today. *"And in thy seed shall all the nations of the earth be blessed: because thou hast obeyed my voice." Genesis 22:18.*

At no time during his enormous test was his wealth ever at issue. In fact, to the original promise given in chapter twelve God now multiplies his descendants into the countless millions, securing father Abraham as the father of many nations. If affected at all, Abraham became richer. It was 100 percent guaranteed. This blessing of universal heritage was all because of his obedience. Verses 17 and 18 of the NLT says *"I will bless you richly; I will multiply your descendants into countless millions, like the stars of the sky and the sand on the seashore. They will conquer their enemies, and through your descendants, all the nations of the earth will be blessed – all because you have obeyed me.*

Sheer obedience is the catalyst to insurmountable blessings. Will your obedience invariably lead to sacrifice? Yes, everyday! The hope is that we won't be asked to literally sacrifice a child or a loved one, yet the reality is - God asks more and more of us each day as we increase in faith and in blessings. In Luke 12:48 we find Jesus as he warns as well as encourages the disciples: *But he that knew not, and did commit things worthy of stripes, shall be beaten with few stripes. For unto whomsoever much is given, of him shall be much required: and to whom men have committed much, of him they will ask the more.* It's the old adage: to whom much is given much is required.

As simple and as uncomplicated as that is, folk insist on complicating the simple truth, when God gives you more he requires more of you. There is no doubting that he gave enormously to Abraham. Yet we remain astounded by his sacrifice. More importantly, God requires a sacrifice of that which you love. No gift or sacrifice is worth giving if it is not first valuable to you. It was the seriousness of sacrifice that made our Lord deliver a cutting edge sermon of what the core of Christianity is. Shortly after He miraculously fed a famished five thousand strong crowd that came to hear him preach –

He said this in Luke 9:23-24: *"If anyone desires to come after Me, let him deny himself, and take up his cross daily, and follow Me. For whoever desires to save his life will lose it, but whoever loses his life for my sake, the same shall save it."*

To that He adds in Matthew 10:37 *"He who loves father or mother more than Me is not worthy of Me. And he who loves son or daughter more than Me is not worthy of Me."*

Wow, the Lord gave us no room for excuses! If we are not committed to even the sacrifice of our families, then forget it – we are not worthy to be called His disciple. No one person, no relationship, and no thing can be excluded from the sacrifice of loss for Christ's sake. But what will be gained is insurmountable.

Centered around the visible and unmistakable wealth of the righteous is the unseen and often overlooked obedience.

In the 15th chapter of First Samuel, when told by the prophet Samuel to destroy the entire Amalekite nation as commanded By the Lord; Saul did his own thing instead. In the 21 verse the prophet reminded Saul of how the Lord specifically instructed him to destroy every man, woman, child, infant, cattle, sheep camel and donkey. Wanting the best of the spoils for himself, he spared the best sheep and cattle claiming them to be reserved for the Lord's sacrifice. Every trace of sin-contaminated flesh was ordered to be wiped out. But King Saul had another agenda, although he would blame his innocent cohorts (his troops) the Prophet Samuel was no dummy – he knew this act of disobedience was Saul's invention – after all, his troops could only act on his command. These were the same troops that he had already commanded to defeat the Amalekite army. And they obeyed his every order. But now the entire nation must be destroyed. Besides his obvious attempt to defraud the prophet, Saul hugely overlooked a hard truth: the God of obedience, and righteousness, would never accept his disgraceful sacrifice of ill repute anyway.

In verse 22 of the NLT The prophet responds to Saul's elaborate cover-up this way: *"What is more pleasing to the Lord: your burnt offerings and sacrifices or your obedience to his voice? Obedience is far better than sacrifice. Listening to Him is far better than the fat of rams. Rebellion is as bad as the sin of witchcraft, and stubbornness is as bad as worshipping idols. So because you have rejected the word of the Lord, He has rejected you from being king."* God is saying the sin of disobedience is as if you practiced witchcraft and worshipped idols – and never worth the consequence of loosing fellowship with Him.

By now I know that you can see that it takes a commitment of obedience and a willingness to sacrifice to live the rich and righteous lifestyle. When Jesus said take up your cross and follow me, He was referring to more than wearing it around your neck. It's one thing to wear a cross and another thing to bear a cross.

Abraham's obedience and sacrifice was strikingly clear, as was Jacob's son Joseph, so was the Shunem woman's, the Canaan woman's and Veronica, the woman with a hemorrhage, theirs was abundantly clear. But none could be clearer than that of our savior's obedience and sacrifice, as none could be richer or more righteous. Obedience and sacrifice is a plight that faces us all. How clear is yours?

As Seen On TV

I'm always intrigued when I hear some young rich accomplished athlete or entertainer say *"I don't want to be anybody's role model"*. That statement has become their buzz catch phrase for the TV cameras. Why not aspire to be a role model? What else is there to accomplish in your mid-twenties and thirties after building multi-million dollar empires, having your face plastered on cereal boxes, and your sneakers being worn by half the teenage population of the modern world?

It's the responsibility of accountability that bewilders these young entrepreneurs. It's not enough to make millions by the hands of those that they so cleverly allude, avoiding the responsibility of being accountable to their wide-eyed audience – while having the *"well, that's just the way the ball bounces"* attitude.

The truth is – we are responsible, and they are responsible. Putting their denial aside, when you are blessed with the rare honor to be in the forefront of any major audience it is because God has allowed your gift to make room for you. It is essential for that room to meet the requirement of morality and righteousness commensurate to that of your gift.

We have become a nation de-sensitized by what we've seen on TV. It is as if the richer they are the less righteous we expect them to be – only holding them accountable for last week's point spread or next year's Grammy nomination. Luke chapter 12 and verse 48 reminds us again that the more you are given the more God expects of you. Yes, the responsibility to shape the minds and consciousness of today's youth is primarily the job of the parents. But our more than fifteen minutes of fame is not without its responsibility too. This is not me pushing religion down any one's throat, this is the balance that I promised you at the beginning of the book.

All of the patriarchs I've highlighted as well as the victorious ben-eficiaries of miracles had to balance their tremendous gifts with a lifestyle in right standing with God.

From Abraham to Jesus Christ, it was understood in the hearts of these nobles that no amount of wealth in the world is worth forfeiting fellowship with the Father. That happens to be the missing ingredient in the lifestyles of our role modeless celebrities. They don't want to be a role model because they can't be a role model. To be fair, it's no fault of their own. They are themselves victims of the same public immorality as seen on TV as much as the youth they so shamelessly avoid. An example of today's new morality is the lesson of health and safety rather than the lesson of spiritual righteousness. Our youth are being taught by television and video exposure the importance of protection from disease and pregnancy during sexual intercourse before marriage. You say – "what's wrong with that, since they're going to do it anyway – shouldn't they practice safe sex?" What's wrong with that is the absence of the real reason to avoid sex before marriage. Because It is a sin against God! Satan, the enemy of our souls has transformed himself into an angel of light and has blinded them into believing in this false sense of righteousness. It's the beautification of sin. It's prettier than calling it fornication when it's all about health and safety. Who could be against this? The scariest part of this fraud is that even well-meaning evangelical Christians have joined the band wagon of giving out condoms and pamphlets for safe sex with a hearty "God bless you".

Any sex outside of the bonds of marriage (ordained by God) can never be safe. We're kidding our selves with this issue of health and safety. It should never come in to play. No amount of condoms in the world can keep fornicators safe from hell's eternal torment.

We've lost sight of the importance of obedience to God's law that declares all fornicators and they that do such things will not inherit the kingdom of God. Galatians 5:21. The lessons of the fear of God have taken a back seat to the lessons that protect our pleasure of sin.

The Prophet Ezekiel as Israel's watchman warned us of this terrible neglect in chapter 33:8 NLT – *"If I announce that some wicked people are sure to die and you fail to warn them about changing their ways, then they will die in their sins, but I will hold you responsible for their deaths. But if you warn them to repent and they don't repent, they will die in their sins, but you will not be held responsible."* As carriers of the Gospel we are watchmen, charged with warning you of the truth.

Our entertainers can't be role models because it would mean telling our youth the truth, even for morality sake if not for righteousness sake. It would mean loosing the support of the easiest, most vulnerable and most gullible supporters of those that see them on TV. When the fear of God over shadows the fear of loosing our target audience which controls the purse strings of our culture – celebrities as all truly anchored Christians, will make a mad dash to be God's chosen role models of truth. Let's be a role model, and do real kingdom work - and tell the truth about sexual immorality and all the other gussied up labels put on the most despicable of sins.

If they want to be like Mike, it means they've been influenced by the riches and wealth they've seen on TV. And certainly, by now you know I have no problem with wealth, God meant for us to be wealthy. What this means for the body of Christ is that we have the responsibility of balancing the desire for the wealth they've seen on the tube with the deep need for a life in right standing with God rarely ever seen on TV.

Chapter Six

CONCLUSION:

Tell It Like It Is...

*P*opular pastor Bishop T. D. Jakes was recently on the cover of Time Magazine as the Billy Graham of his time. His Dallas, Texas based ministry caters to a membership in the several thousands and he is seen on television around the world. If his flair for dressing is any indication of his lifestyle, Bishop Jakes is undoubtedly living the lifestyles of the Rich and Righteous. Dr. Creflo Dollar, Pastor Joel Olsteen, Dr. Joyce Meyer and one of my favorites Marilyn Hickey, along with many others also have large ministries reaching millions by television around the world, and have accumulated huge followings.

There are many more that I have not mentioned as well as those that serve diligently in obscurity, that I give a salute to.

By the sound of things it may appear that there is little or no need for more preachers especially on television. Believe it or not even more is needed. Until we have as many or more television preachers as the world has in perverse pontificators as seen on T.V. – then we haven't begun to scratch the surface. Just to be clear, there is no race to compete with secular television just for the sake of competition. Although, there is a haste to overwhelm the perverseness that has desensitized a self-seeking world towards Godlessness. If we believe the statistics and the numbers being reported, then half of the globe are born-again Christians. But the numbers have been hugely over reported. That statistic just doesn't hold true with the scriptures – which means we have way more work to do.

In Matthew 7:13-14 NLT Jesus poignantly reveals the facts of the real census. With frightening accuracy He proves that these statistics can't be true. He reports it this way: *"You can enter God's Kingdom only through the narrow gate. The Highway to hell is broad, and its gate is wide for the many who choose the easy way. But the gateway to life is small, and the road is narrow, and only a few ever find it."*

The reports of billions of Christians world wide sounds more like the other gate. According to what Jesus said, the narrow gate isn't that crowded. Frankly the narrow gate is not the reason so many of us have a lot of work to do. It's actually that wide or broad gate that makes us strongly aware that we have much more work to do. Those of us that are charged with teaching the Biblical truth dare to try to rescue those in the comfort zone of the broad road. There are simply too many people on that road for us to let up. We also know that the altering affects of the Gospel as commanded in Mark 16:15-16 is the only thing to remedy their condition.

Fortunately for them evangelism is on the rise. The church of today has been blessed with the technology of this modern age. Every medium available is being used to reach the lost at any cost. Television, radio, books, videos, cassettes, CDs and now DVDs distributed across the globe. Before Jesus comes back, we had better have gone forth, meeting the demands of His charge to us in the Gospel of Mark.

We must justly level the need for world wide evangelism with the need for wealth in the body of Christ. I've talked about wealth and righteousness a great deal – in order to balance your understanding of the need for both. However, the wealth required for the body of

Christ to expand the Gospel is critical. The dreaded truth is that the church needs and ABUNDANCE of wealth to carry out the instructions given by Jesus Christ. He knew this when He placed the order for us to go into all the world. Every charge He ever gave was to challenge our faith - this was no different. Now, more than ever before we have the ability to reach out to every corner of the universe and save (at least some) lost on that broad road. They are in China, Malaysia, Pakistan, Ethiopia, South Africa, Ghana, Kenya, Canada, Australia, Croatia, Central America, Honduras, Belize, Mexico, The Caribbean and the world, and it will take the faith that I have shown you as well as the wealth, to reach them.

The charge is individually ours as well as it is collectively ours. So it is not for us to sit back and relax and say "let Paul and Jan handle it – they know what to do". Now so do you. I have attempted to build your faith not just for your own personal mission, but for the greater mission. Of the greatest concern to us should be keeping the charge of saving lost souls - by extending the Gospel to the furthest corners of the earth. This is how we will advance His Kingdom, and this is the greatest mission.

As we look back on everything the Lord has allowed me to reveal, I pray that I have been able to enlighten you in the area of the church and prosperity. It was my mission to bridge the gap in people's minds between the two – as well as give you direction for your life. And, as promised, balance the understanding of the word of God concerning wealth and righteousness. If you have continued with me up to this point I'm confident that you now know the truth. The seldom spoken, hard to accept truth, is that the richest man that ever lived paid an immeasurable price for the righteous to live rich while advancing the kingdom of God - while in this earth. That same price was paid as our ransom to guarantee that we would never live spiritually bankrupt again. His suffering and inevitable death and resurrection is our assurance that we can have them both. Live long and prosper!

ABOUT THE AUTHOR

*D*r. Katrine Forbes is founder, senior pastor and teacher of Now Faith Ministries Miami, Florida. The founding overseer of Now Faith Ministry satellites nationally, in Houston Texas, Augusta Georgia, Las Vegas Nevada and Miami, Fl. Dr. Forbes is responsible for birthing many of today's influential leaders in the full Gospel arena. The creator and developer of Divine Favor and Words of Wisdom television and international radio broadcasts.

One of today's foremost preachers of the Bible, Dr. Forbes' revelatory style of teaching exposes hearers to the Gospel truth through divine revelation, empowering the faith that changes life's circumstances. Dr. Forbes and her husband, Elder David Forbes Sr. are blessed with ten adult biological children, Fourteen grandchildren and four great grandchildren. Through over forty five years of commitment to ministry, Dr. Forbes has birthed thousands of spiritual children.

For more details about Dr. Forbes and other resources of her teachings and ministries, please contact:

NOW FAITH MINISTRIES
9275 NW 32 AVENUE
MIAMI, FLORIDA 33147.
Or Call: 305-694-9631